FIRST 50 SONGS

YOU SHOULD PLAY ON UKULELE

ISBN 978-1-4950-3112-0

HAL•LEONARD®
CORPORATION
7777 W. BLUEMOUND RD. P.O. BOX 13819 MILWAUKEE, WI 53213

Visit Hal Leonard Online at
www.halleonard.com

CONTENTS

Amazing Grace

Words by John Newton
Traditional American Melody

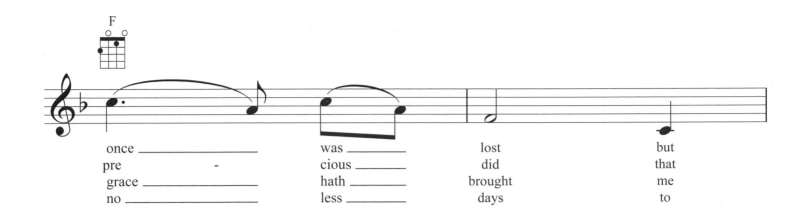

once _____	was _____	lost	but
pre -	cious _____	did	that
grace _____	hath _____	brought	me
no _____	less _____	days	to

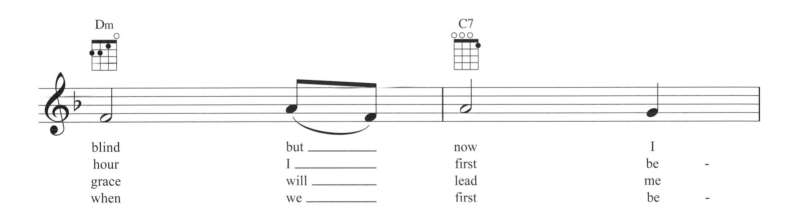

now _____	am _____	found,	was
grace _____	ap -	pear	the
safe _____	thus _____	far,	and
sing _____	God's _____	praise	than

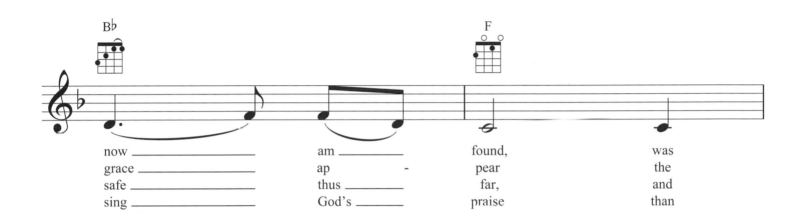

blind	but _____	now	I
hour	I _____	first	be -
grace	will _____	lead	me
when	we _____	first	be -

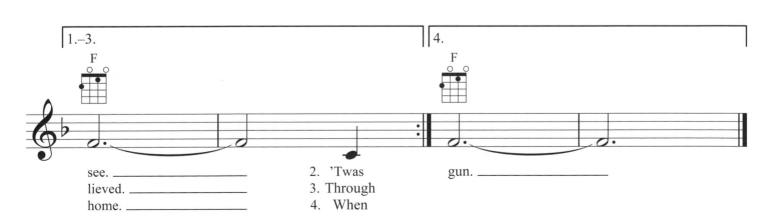

1.–3.

see. _____	2. 'Twas
lieved. _____	3. Through
home. _____	4. When

4.

gun. _____

Auld Lang Syne

Words by Robert Burns
Traditional Scottish Melody

Afternoon Delight

Words and Music by Bill Danoff

2., 4. Think-ing of you's work-ing up my ap - pe - tite, look-ing for-ward to a lit-tle af - ter-
(3.) out __ this __ morn-ing feel-ing so po - lite. I al-ways thought a fish could not be caught who

noon de - light. __ Rub-bing sticks and stones to - geth - er make the sparks ig - nite, and the
did - n't bite. __ But you got some bait a - wait-ing and I think I might like __

Chorus

thought of rub-bing you is get-ting so ex - cit - ing. ⎫ Sky rock-ets in flight,
nib - bl-ing a lit-tle af - ter - noon de - light. __ ⎭

af - ter - noon __ de -light, af -

- ter - noon __ de - light, af -

To Coda ⊕

1.

2.

- ter - noon __ de - light. _____ 3. Start - ed

8

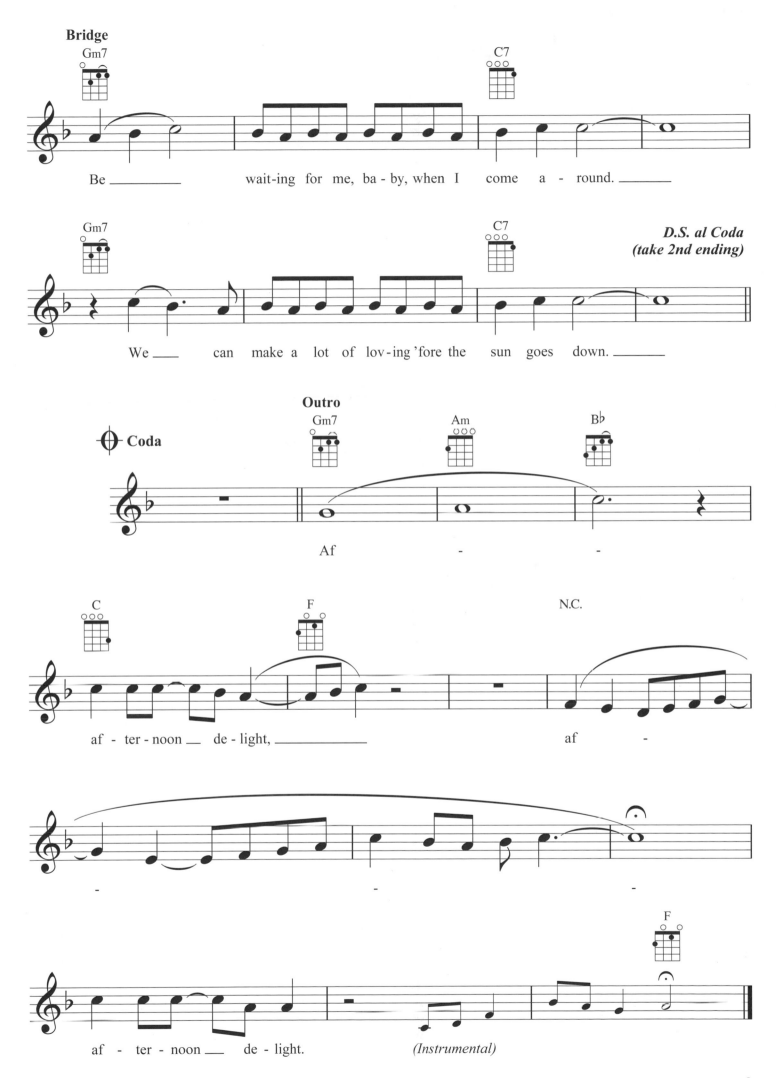

Bridge

Gm7   C7

Be _____ wait-ing for me, ba - by, when I come a - round. _____

Gm7   C7   *D.S. al Coda*
                                                                   (take 2nd ending)

We ___ can make a lot of lov-ing 'fore the sun goes down. _____

Outro

Coda   Gm7   Am   Bb

Af - -

C   F   N.C.

af - ter - noon __ de - light, _____   af -

-   -   -

                                                                                            F

af - ter - noon __ de - light.   *(Instrumental)*

Blowin' in the Wind

Words and Music by Bob Dylan

Additional Lyrics

2. How many years can a mountain exist
   Before it is washed to the sea?
   How many years can some people exist
   Before they're allowed to be free?
   Yes, and how many times can a man turn his head
   And pretend that he just doesn't see?

3. How many times must a man look up
   Before he can see the sky?
   How many ears must one man have
   Before he can hear people cry?
   Yes, and how many deaths will it take till he knows
   That too many people have died?

Both Sides Now

Words and Music by Joni Mitchell

1. Bows and flows of an - gel hair ___ and

2., 3. *See additional lyrics*

ice cream cas - tles ___ in the air, ___ and

feath - ered can - yons ev - 'ry - where; ___

I've looked at clouds that way. But

now they on - ly block ___ the sun. ___ They

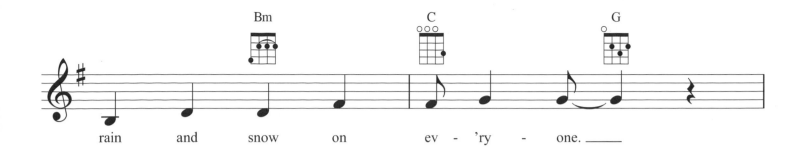

rain and snow on ev - 'ry - one. ____

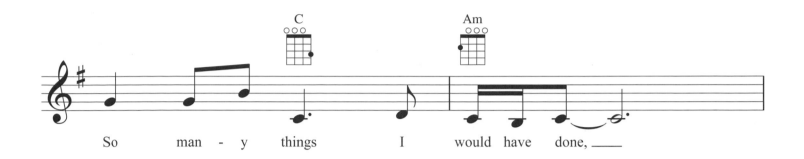

So man - y things I would have done, ____

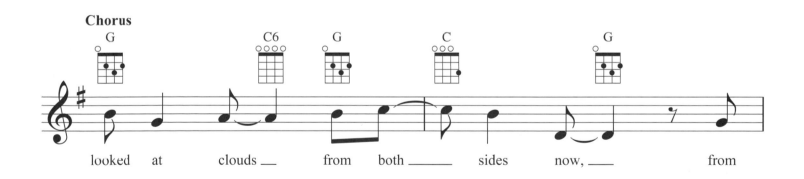

but clouds ____ got in my ____ way. I've

Chorus

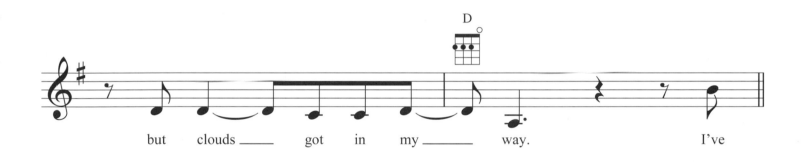

looked at clouds ____ from both ____ sides now, ____ from

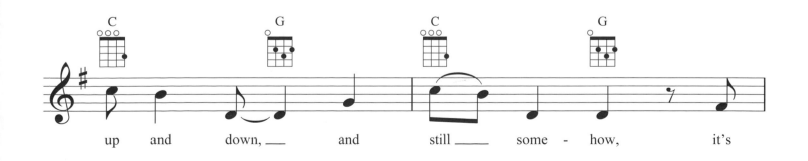

up and down, ___ and still ____ some - how, it's

clouds' il - lu - sions I re - call. ___ I real - ly don't know

clouds ___ at ___ all. ___

Additional Lyrics

2. Moons and Junes and Ferris wheels,
   The dizzy dancing way you feel
   When ev'ry fairy tale comes real;
   I've looked at love that way.
   But now it's just another show.
   You leave 'em laughing when you go.
   And if you care, don't let them know,
   Don't give yourself away.

Chorus: I've looked at love from both sides now,
   From win and lose, and still somehow,
   It's love's illusions I recall.
   I really don't know love at all.

3. Tears and fears and feeling proud
   To say, "I love you" right out loud,
   Dreams and schemes and circus crowds;
   I've looked at life that way.
   But now old friends are acting strange.
   They shake their heads, they say I've changed.
   Well, something's lost and something's gained
   In living ev'ry day.

Chorus: I've looked at life from both sides now,
   From give and take, and still somehow,
   It's life's illusions I recall.
   I really don't know life at all.

Boulevard of Broken Dreams

Words by Billie Joe
Music by Green Day

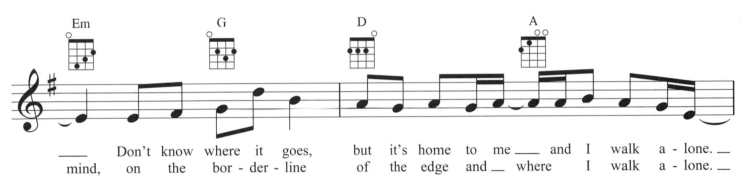

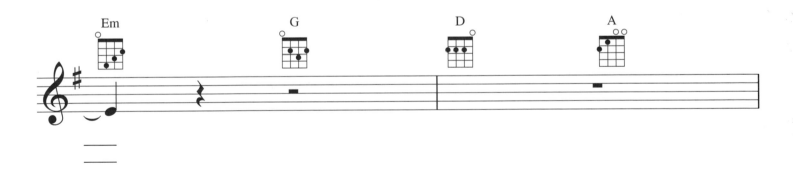

(Sittin' On)
The Dock of the Bay

Words and Music by Steve Cropper and Otis Redding

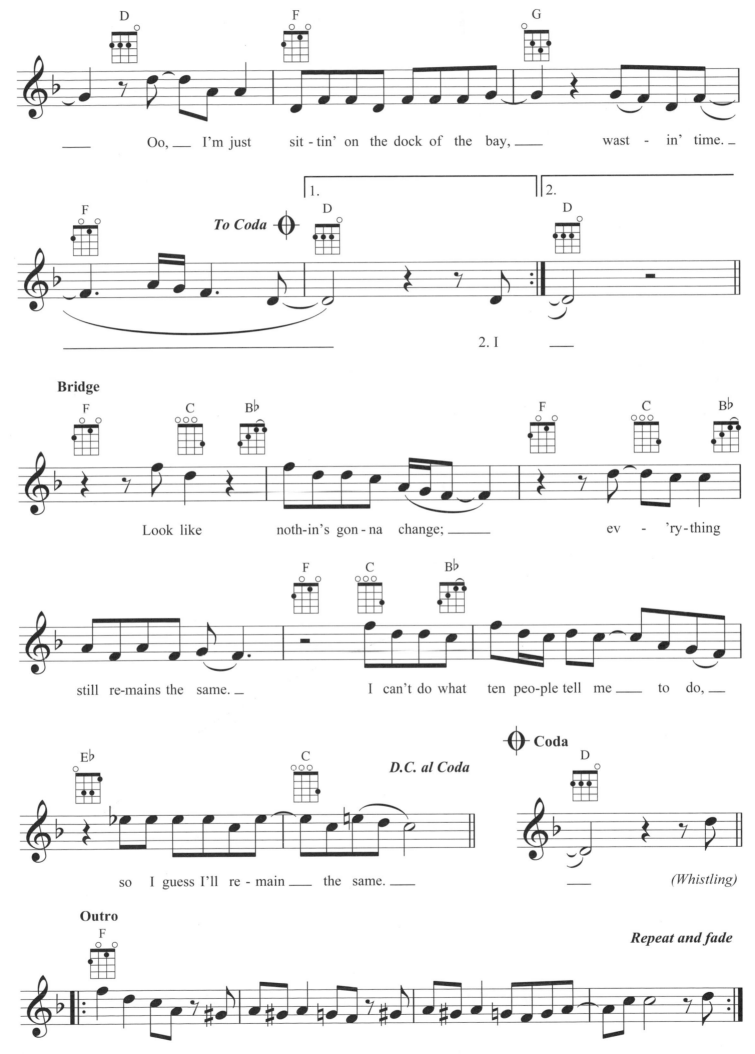

Edelweiss

from THE SOUND OF MUSIC
Lyrics by Oscar Hammerstein II
Music by Richard Rodgers

Bridge

Blos - som of snow, may you bloom and

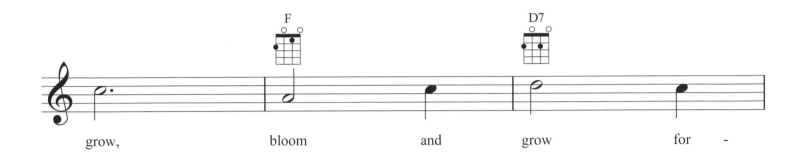

grow, bloom and grow for -

Chorus

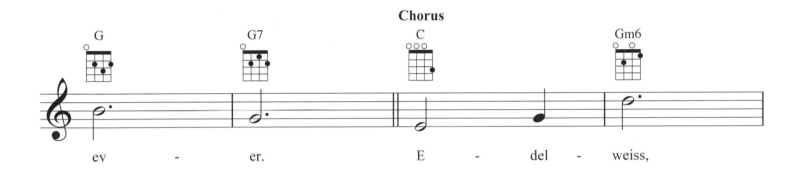

ev - er. E - del - weiss,

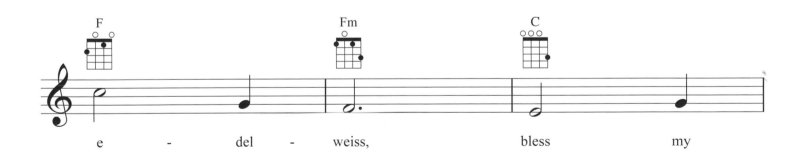

e - del - weiss, bless my

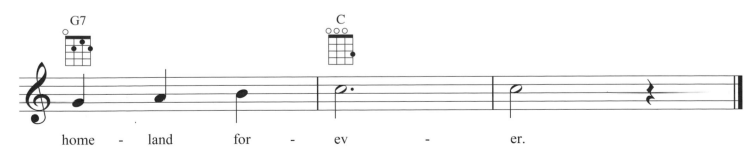

home - land for - ev - er.

Everything Is Beautiful

Words and Music by Ray Stevens

sum - mer night or a snow - cov - ered win - ter's

day. Ev - 'ry - bod - y's beau - ti - ful _____ in their own

way. _____ Un - der God's heav - en, the

To Coda

world's gon - na find _____ a way. _____

Verse

1. There is none so blind _____ as he who will not
2. *See additional lyrics*

see. _____ We must not close our minds, _____ we must

Additional Lyrics

2. We shouldn't care about the length of his hair or the color of his skin.
   Don't worry about what shows from without but the love that lies within.
   We gonna get it all together now and everything's gonna work out fine.
   Just take a little time to look on the good side, my friend, and straighten it out in your mind.

Escape
(The Piña Colada Song)
Words and Music by Rupert Holmes

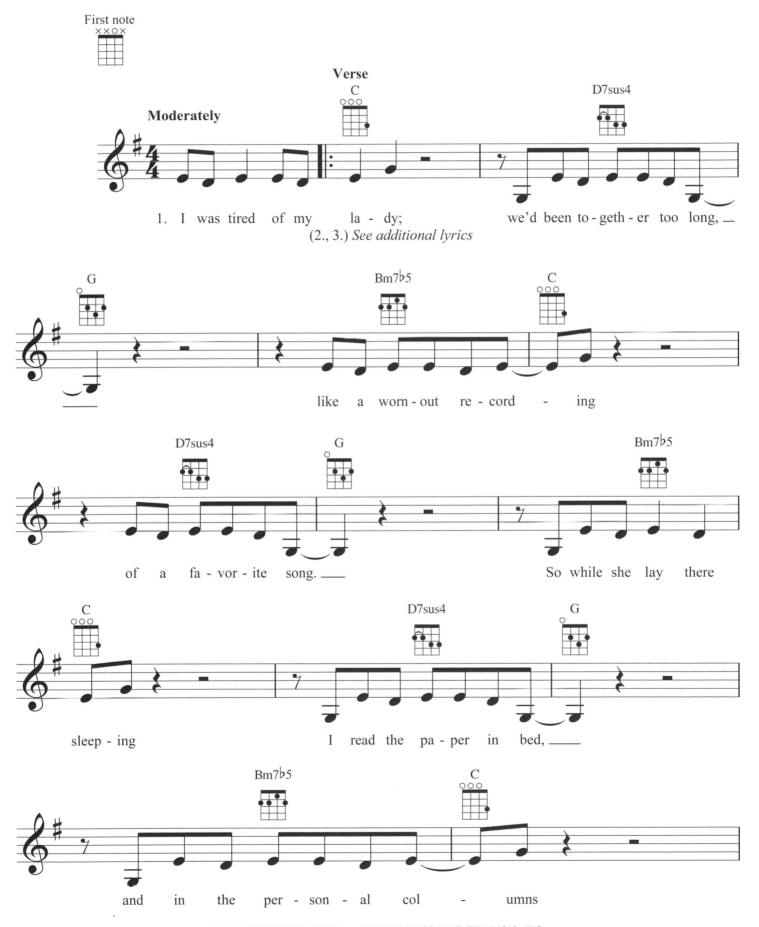

1. I was tired of my la - dy; we'd been to - geth - er too long, _____

(2., 3.) See additional lyrics

like a worn - out re - cord - ing of a fa - vor - ite song. _____ So while she lay there

sleep - ing I read the pa - per in bed, _____

and in the per - son - al col - umns

there was this let - ter I read: ____ "If you like pi - ña co -

Chorus

la - das and get - ting caught in the rain,

if you're not in - to yo - ga, if you have half a

brain, if you'd like mak - ing love at

mid - night ____ in the dunes on the Cape,

then I'm the love that you've looked for.

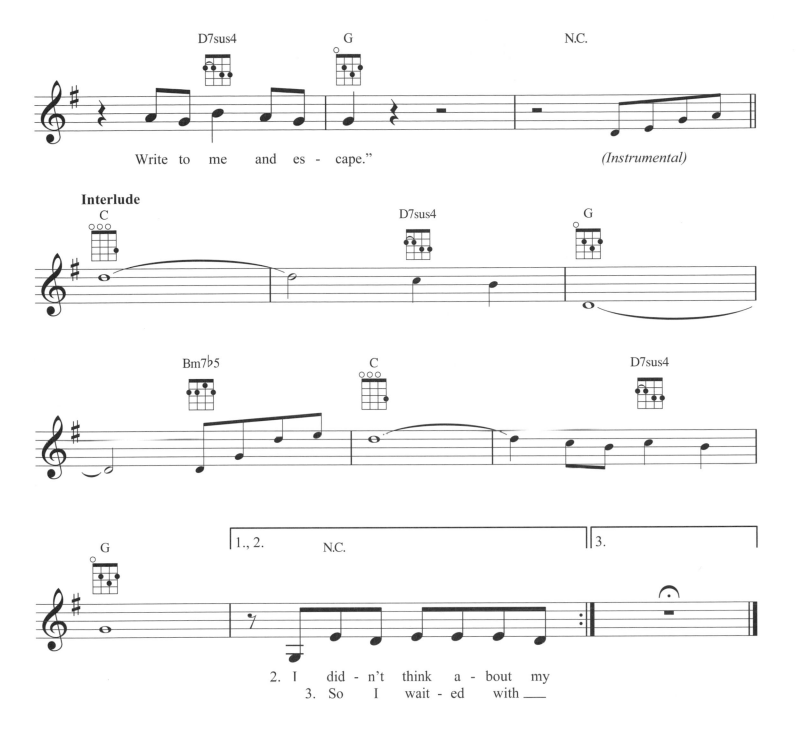

Additional Lyrics

2. I didn't think about my lady; I know that sounds kinda mean.
   But me and my old lady have fallen into the same old dull routine.
   So I wrote to the paper, took out a personal ad.
   And though I'm nobody's poet, I thought it wasn't half bad:
   "Yes, I like piña coladas and getting caught in the rain.
   I'm not much into health food; I am into champagne.
   I've got to meet you by tomorrow noon and cut through all this red tape,
   At a bar called O'Malley's, where we'll plan our escape."

3. So I waited with high hopes, and she walked in the place.
   I knew her smile in an instant, I knew the curve of her face.
   It was my own lovely lady, and she said, "Oh, it's you!"
   Then we laughed for a moment, and I said, "I never knew
   That you like piña coladas and getting caught in the rain,
   And the feel of the ocean and the taste of champagne.
   If you'd like making love at midnight in the dunes on the Cape,
   You're the lady I've looked for. Come with me and escape."

Gentle on My Mind

Words and Music by John Hartford

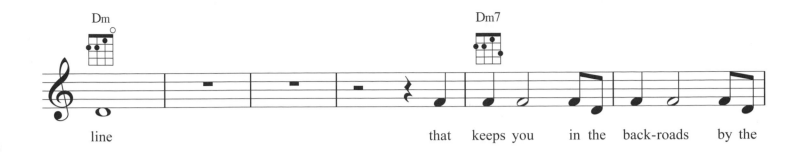

line

riv-ers   of   my   mem-'ry   that   keeps   you   ev-er   gen-tle   on   my

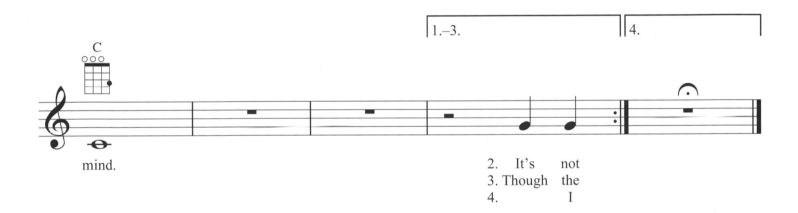

mind.

2. It's   not
3. Though   the
4.   I

Additional Lyrics

2. It's not clinging to the rocks and ivy planted on their columns now that bind me,
   Or something that somebody said because they thought we fit together walkin'.
   It's just knowing that the world will not be cursing or forgiving when I walk along some railroad track and find
   That you're moving on the backroad by the rivers of my memory, and for hours you're just gentle on my mind.

3. Though the wheat fields and the clotheslines and the junkyards and the highways come between us,
   And some other woman's crying to her mother 'cause she turned and I was gone.
   I still might run in silence, tears of joy might stain my face and the summer sun might burn me 'til I'm blind,
   But not to where I cannot see you walkin' on the backroads by the rivers flowing gentle on my mind.

4. I dip my cup of soup back from a gurglin', cracklin' caldron in some train yard,
   My beard a roughening coal pile and a dirty hat pulled low across my face.
   Through cupped hands 'round the tin can I pretend I hold you to my breast and find
   That you're waiting from the backroads by the rivers of my memory, ever smilin', ever gentle on my mind.

Hallelujah

Words and Music by Leonard Cohen

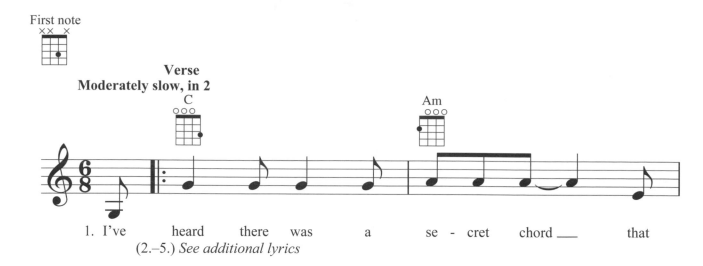

1. I've heard there was a se - cret chord ___ that
(2.–5.) *See additional lyrics*

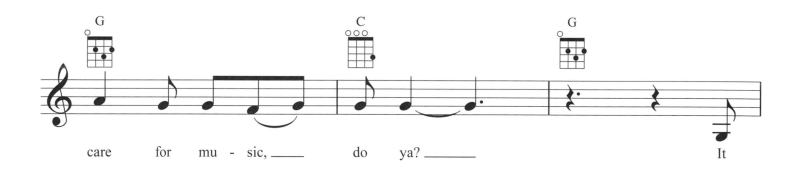

Da - vid played ___ and it pleased the Lord, ___ but you don't ___ real - ly

care for mu - sic, ___ do ya? ___ It

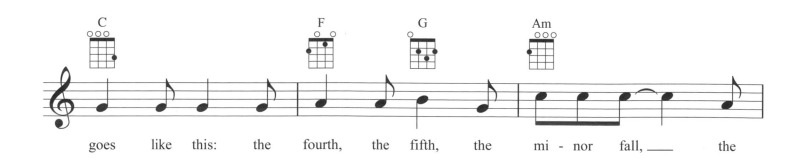

goes like this: the fourth, the fifth, the mi - nor fall, ___ the

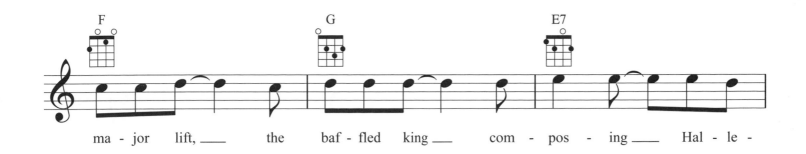

ma - jor lift, _____ the baf - fled king _____ com - pos - ing _____ Hal - le -

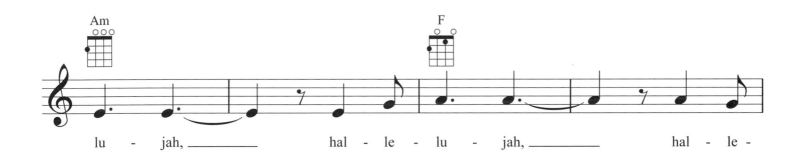

Chorus

lu - jah. _____ Hal - le - lu - jah, _____ hal - le -

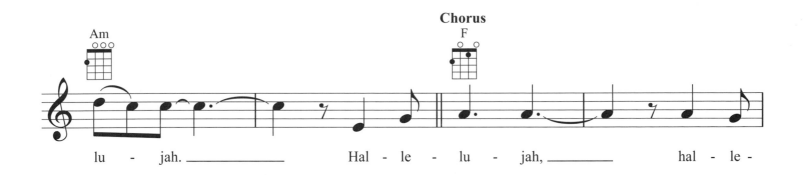

lu - jah, _____ hal - le - lu - jah, _____ hal - le -

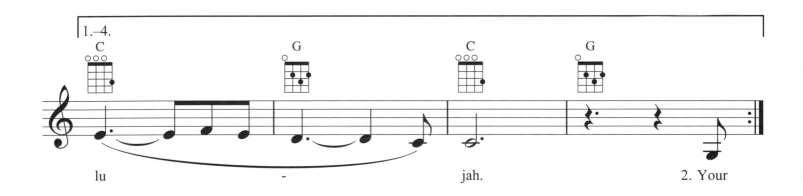

1.–4.

lu - jah. 2. Your

5.

Outro-Chorus

lu - jah. Hal - le - lu - jah. _____ Hal - le -

lu - jah. _____   Hal - le - lu - jah. _____   Hal - le -

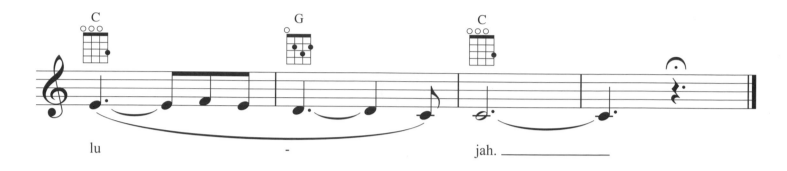

lu   -   jah. _____

Additional Lyrics

2. Your faith was strong but you needed proof.
   You saw her bathing on the roof.
   Her beauty and the moonlight overthrew ya.
   She tied you to a kitchen chair.
   She broke your throne, she cut your hair.
   And from your lips she drew the Hallelujah.

3. Maybe I have been here before.
   I know this room, I've walked this floor.
   I used to live alone before I knew ya.
   I've seen your flag on the marble arch.
   Love is not a vict'ry march.
   It's a cold and it's a broken Hallelujah.

4. There was a time you let me know
   What's real and going on below.
   But now you never show it to me, do ya?
   And remember when I moved in you.
   The holy dark was movin', too,
   And every breath we drew was Hallelujah.

5. Maybe there's a God above,
   And all I ever learned from love
   Was how to shoot at someone who outdrew ya.
   And it's not a cry you can hear at night.
   It's not somebody who's seen the light.
   It's a cold and it's a broken Hallelujah.

The 59th Street Bridge Song

(Feelin' Groovy)

Words and Music by Paul Simon

First note

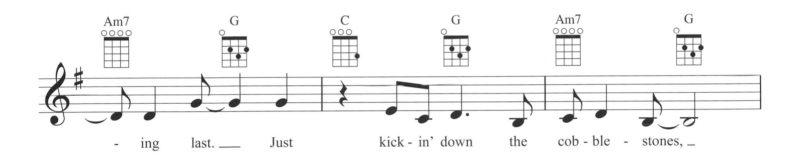

1. Slow down, __ you move too fast. __ You got to make the morn-

- ing last. __ Just kick - in' down the cob - ble - stones, __

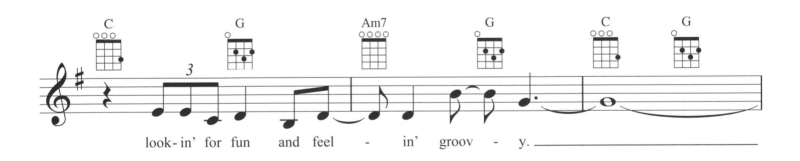

look - in' for fun and feel - in' groov - y. __

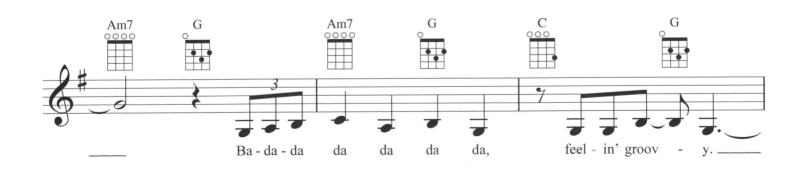

__ Ba - da - da da da da da, feel - in' groov - y. __

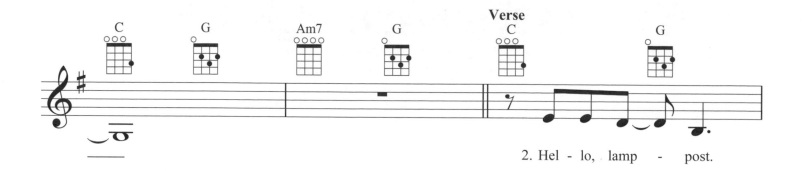

Verse

2. Hel - lo, lamp - post.

What - cha know - in'? I've come to watch your flow - ers grow - in'.

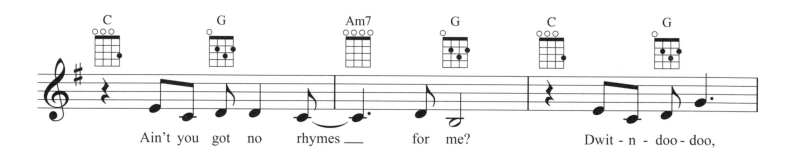

Ain't you got no rhymes ___ for me? Dwit - n - doo - doo,

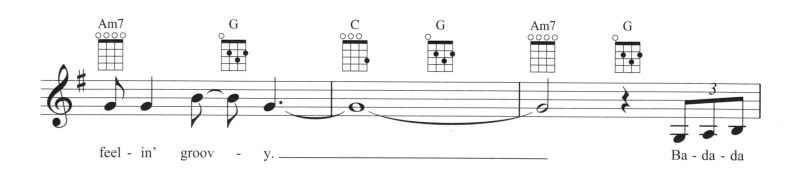

feel - in' groov - y. _____ Ba - da - da

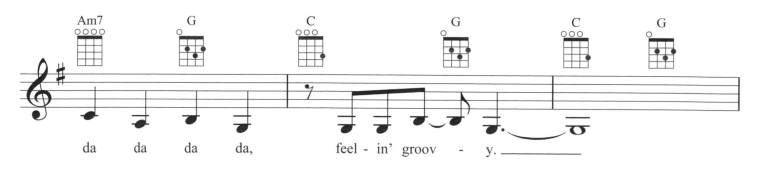

da da da da, feel - in' groov - y. _____

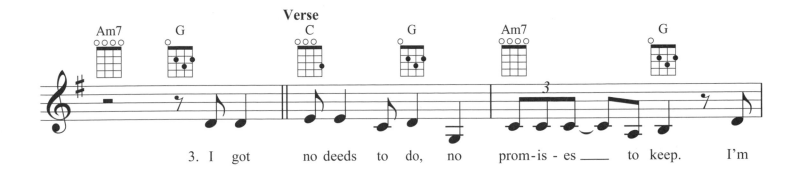

3. I got no deeds to do, no prom-is-es ___ to keep. I'm

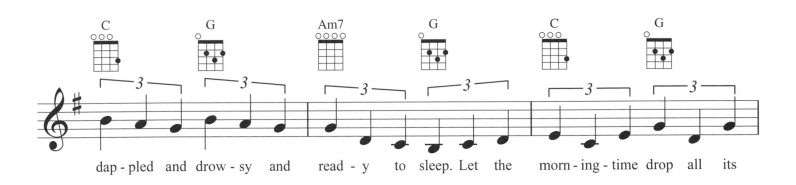

dap-pled and drow-sy and read-y to sleep. Let the morn-ing-time drop all its

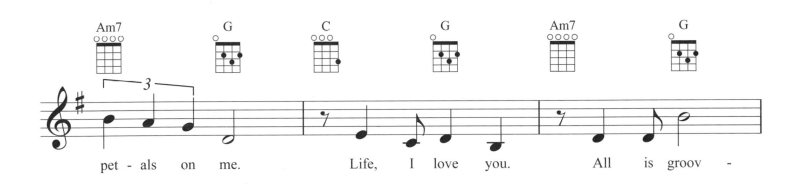

pet-als on me. Life, I love you. All is groov-

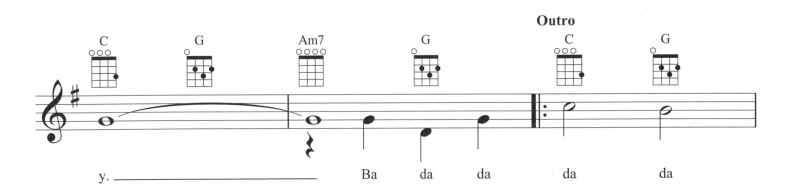

Outro

y. ___ Ba da da da da

Repeat and fade

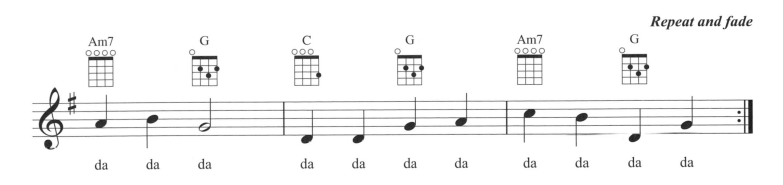

da da da da da da da da da da da

Happy Together

Words and Music by Garry Bonner and Alan Gordon

day and night. It's on-ly right to think a-bout the girl you love and hold her

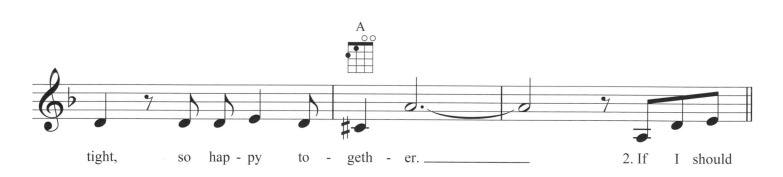

tight, so hap-py to-geth-er. _____ 2. If I should

call you up, in-vest a dime, and you say you be-long to me and ease my

3., 4. Me and you and you and me. No mat-ter how they tossed the dice, it had to

Hey, Soul Sister

Words and Music by Pat Monahan, Espen Lind and Amund Bjorklund

* Originally recorded in E major.

1.

Interlude

F   G   C

thing you do _____ to - night. ____ Hey, __

G   Am   F

__ hey, _____ hey. _____

2.

Bridge

G   C

____ to - night. ____ The way you can cut a rug, __

G   Am

watch-ing you's __ the on - ly drug __ I need. __ Some gang - sta, I'm __ so thug. __ You're the

F   C

on - ly one ___ I'm dream - in' of. ___ You see, I can be my - self now, fi - nal - ly.

G   Am

In fact, __ there's noth - in' I _____ can't be. ___ I want the world to see ___ you'll

40

Additional Lyrics

2. Just in time, I'm so glad you have a one-track mind like me.
   You gave my life direction,
   A game-show love connection we can't deny.
   I'm so obsessed, my heart is bound to beat right out my untrimmed chest.
   I believe in you. Like a virgin, you're Madonna
   And I'm always gonna wanna blow your mind.

I Walk the Line

Words and Music by John R. Cash

First note

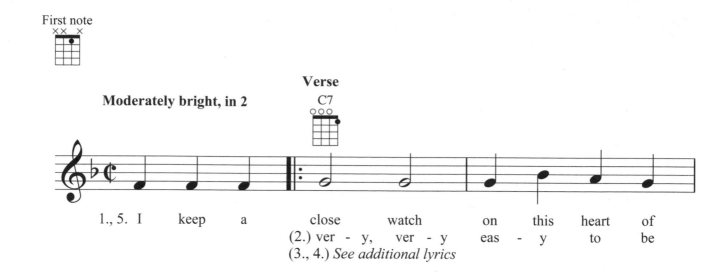

Moderately bright, in 2

Verse

1., 5. I keep a close watch on this heart of
(2.) ver - y, ver - y eas - y to be
(3., 4.) *See additional lyrics*

mine. _____ I keep my eyes wide
true. _____ I find my - self a - lone

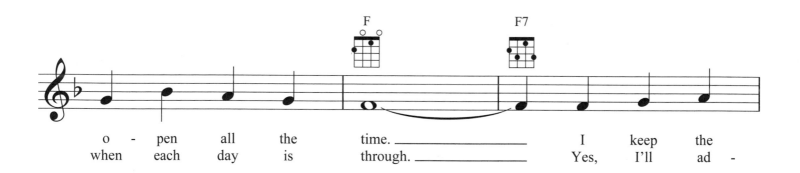

o - pen all the time. _____ I keep the
when each day is through. _____ Yes, I'll ad -

ends out for the tie that binds. _____
mit that I'm a fool for you. _____

Be - cause you're mine, ___

I walk the line. ___

2. I find it line. ___
3. As sure as
4. You've got a

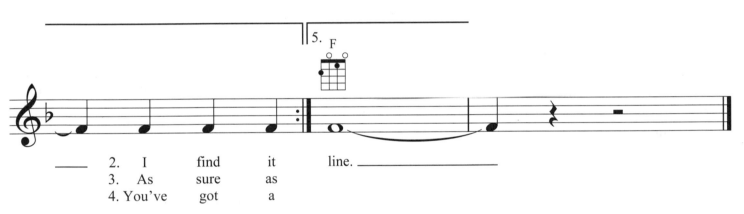

Additional Lyrics

3. As sure as night is dark and day is light,
   I keep you on my mind both day and night.
   And happiness I've known proves that it's right.
   Because you're mine, I walk the line.

4. You've got a way to keep me on your side.
   You give me a cause for love that I can't hide.
   For you I know I'd even try to turn the tide.
   Because you're mine, I walk the line.

I'd Like to Teach the World to Sing

Words and Music by Bill Backer, Roquel Davis, Roger Cook and Roger Greenaway

1. I'd like to build the world a home and
(2., 3.) *See additional lyrics*

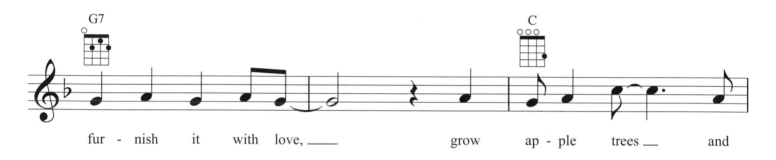

fur - nish it with love, grow ap - ple trees and

hon - ey bees and snow - white tur - tle - doves. 2. I'd

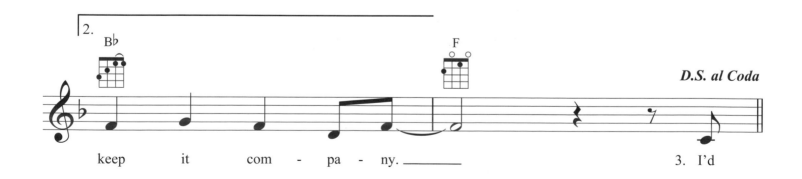

keep it com - pa - ny. 3. I'd

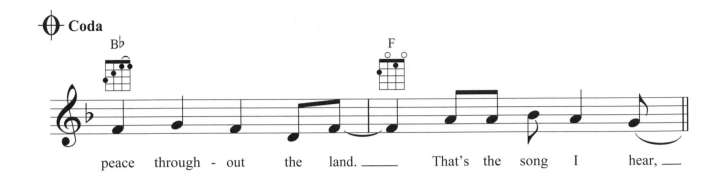

peace through - out the land. _____ That's the song I hear, ___

Bridge

_____ let the world sing to - day.

Outro

I'd like to teach ___ the world ___ to sing ___ in

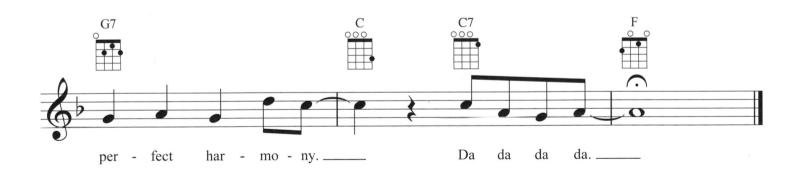

per - fect har - mo - ny. _____ Da da da da. _____

Additional Lyrics

2. I'd like to teach the world to sing in perfect harmony.
   I'd like to hold it in my arms and keep it company.

3. I'd like to see the world, for once, all standing hand in hand,
   And hear them echo through the hills for peace throughout the land.

I'm Yours

Words and Music by Jason Mraz

reck-on it's a-gain my turn _____ to win some ___ or learn some. But
what we aim to do. Our name is _____ our vir - tue.

Chorus

I won't hes - i - tate no more, no more. It

To Coda

can - not wait. I'm yours. _____

Bridge

2. Well, o - pen up your mind and see ___ like me. ___ O - pen up your

plans and, damn, __ you're free. ___ Look in - to your heart and you'll __ find

love,   love, _____ love,   love.   Lis - ten to the mu - sic of the

mo - ment; peo - ple dance _ and   sing.   We're just one big fam - i - ly, _

_____   and it's our god - for - sak - en right to be   loved,   loved, _____

loved,   loved,   loved. _____   So,

Chorus

I   won't   hes - i - tate   no   more,   no

more.   It   can - not   wait.   I'm   sure _____ there's no

48

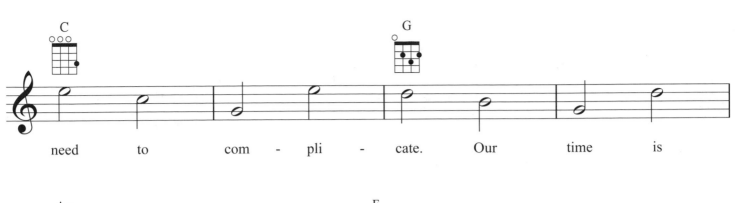

need to com - pli - cate. Our time is

short. This is our fate. I'm yours. _____ Scat...

Interlude

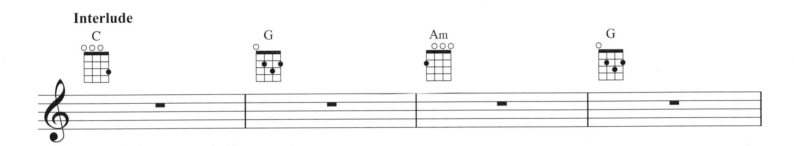

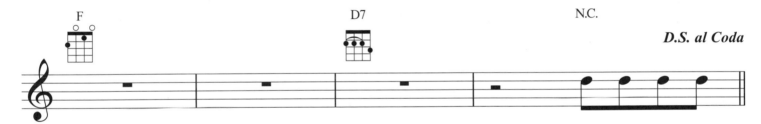

D.S. al Coda

3. I've been spend-ing

Coda　　　　　　**Bridge/Chorus**

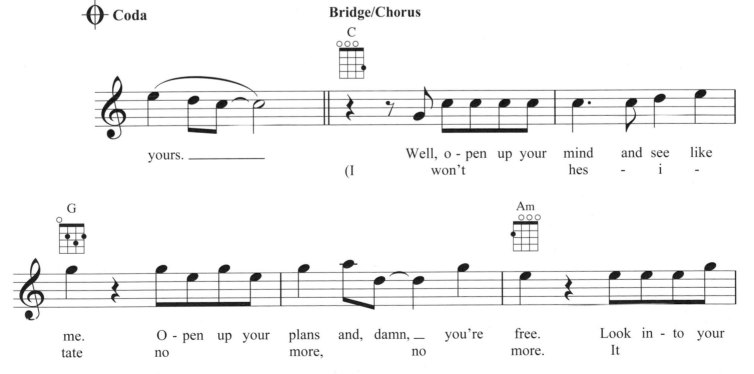

yours. _____ 　　(I

Well, o - pen up your mind and see like
won't hes - i -

me.　　O - pen up your plans and, damn,_ you're free. Look in - to your
tate　no　　more,　　no　　more.　It

heart and you'll _ find that the sky is yours. _____ So,
can - not wait I'm sure. _____ No

please don't, please don't, please don't... There's no need _ to com - pli -
need to com - pli - cate. Our

cate 'cause our time is short. _ This is, this is, this is our
time is short. This is our

fate. I'm yours. _____ Scat...
fate. I'm yours.) _____

Outro

Repeat and fade

Imagine

Words and Music by John Lennon

Chorus

you may say _____ I'm a dream-er, but I'm not the on-ly one. I hope some day _____ you'll join us _____ and the world _____ will

1. be as one. ____

2. live as one. ____

Additional Lyrics

3. Imagine no possessions,
   I wonder if you can;
   No need for greed or hunger,
   A brotherhood of man.
   Imagine all the people sharing all the world.

If I Had a Hammer
(The Hammer Song)

Words and Music by Lee Hays and Pete Seeger

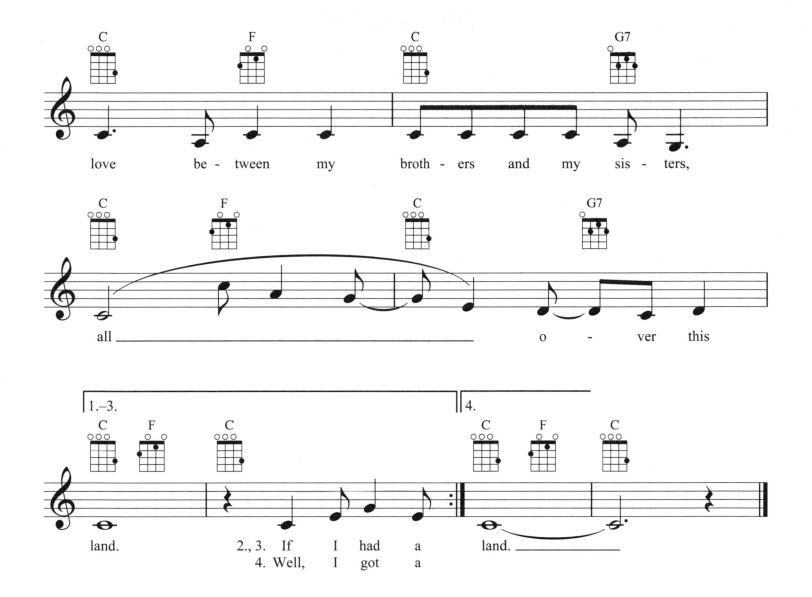

Additional Lyrics

2. If I had a bell, I'd ring it in the morning,
   I'd ring it in the evening all over this land.
   I'd ring out danger, I'd ring out a warning,
   I'd ring out love between my brothers and my sisters,
   All over this land.

3. If I had a song, I'd sing it in the morning,
   I'd sing it in the evening all over this land.
   I'd sing out danger, I'd sing out a warning,
   I'd sing out love between my brothers and my sisters,
   All over this land.

4. Well, I got a hammer, and I've got a bell,
   And I've got a song to sing all over this land.
   It's the hammer of justice, it's the bell of freedom,
   It's the song about love between my brothers and my sisters,
   All over this land.

Jambalaya
(On the Bayou)

Words and Music by Hank Williams

Chorus

Jam - ba - la - ya, and a craw - fish pie, and fil - let gum - bo. _____ 'Cause to - night I'm gon - na see my ma cher a mi - o. _____ Pick gui - tar, ____ fill fruit jar, and be gay - o. _____ Son of a gun, we'll have big fun on the bay - ou. _____ 2. Thi - bo - _____

Love Me Tender

Words and Music by Elvis Presley and Vera Matson

Leaving on a Jet Plane

Words and Music by John Denver

blow - in' his horn. __ Al - read - y I'm so lone - some I could
sing for you. __ When I come back so I'll bring your wed - ding
leave a - lone, __ a - bout the times I won't have to

Chorus

die. _____ So kiss ⎫
ring. _____ So kiss ⎬ me and smile for me, __
say: _____ Kiss ⎭

tell me that __ you'll wait for me, __ hold me like __ you'll

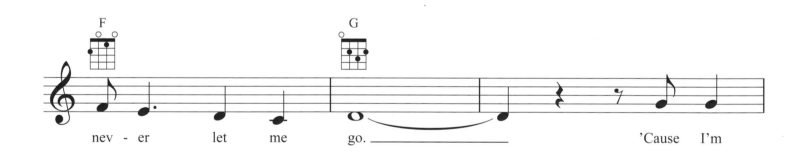

nev - er let me go. _____ 'Cause I'm

leav - in' on a jet __ plane, don't know when

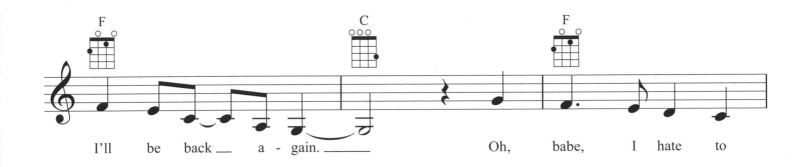

I'll be back __ a - gain. _____ Oh, babe, I hate to

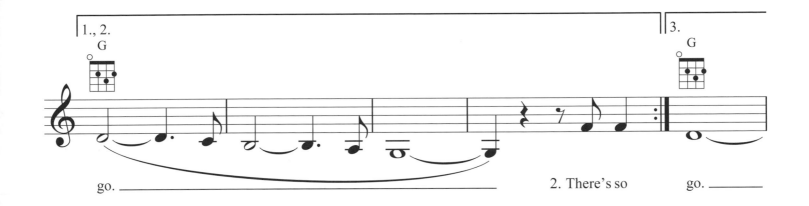

1., 2.

3.

go. _____ 2. There's so go. _____

Outro

___ I'm leav - in' on a jet __ plane, don't know when

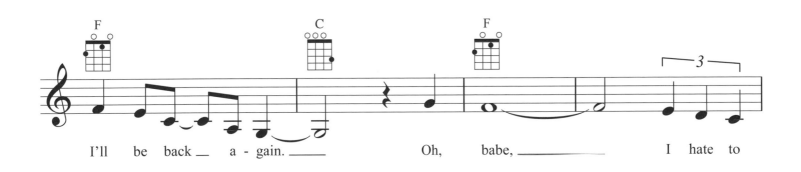

I'll be back __ a - gain. ___ Oh, babe, _____ I hate to

go. _____

Mack the Knife

from THE THREEPENNY OPERA

English Words by Marc Blitzstein
Original German Words by Bert Brecht
Music by Kurt Weill

First note

Verse
Moderately, in 2

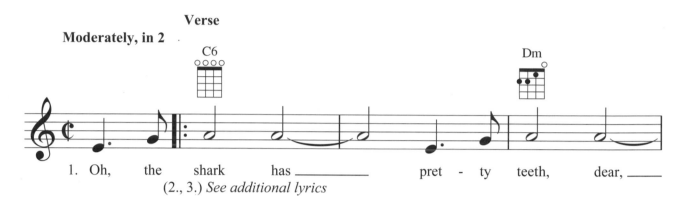

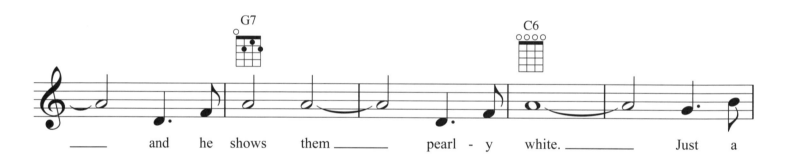

1. Oh, the shark has _____ pret - ty teeth, dear, _____
(2., 3.) *See additional lyrics*

_____ and he shows them _____ pearl - y white. _____ Just a

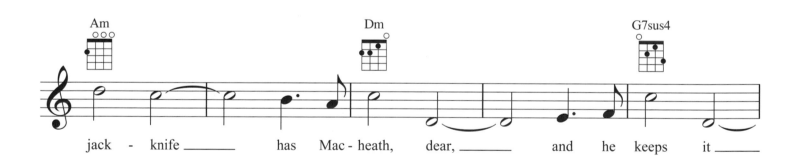

jack - knife _____ has Mac - heath, dear, _____ and he keeps it

_____ out of sight. _____ When the shark bites _____ with his

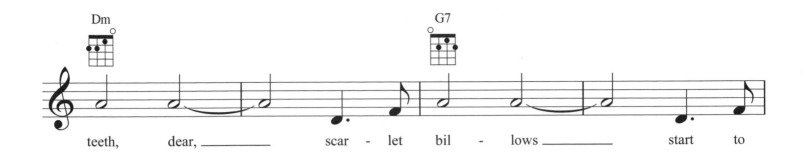

teeth,   dear, _____   scar - let bil - lows _____ start to

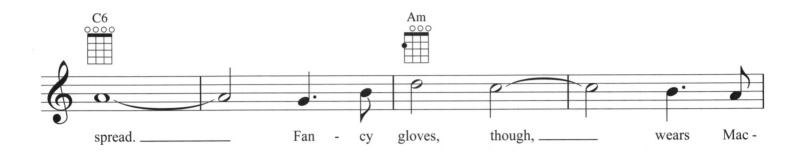

spread. _____   Fan - cy gloves, though, _____ wears Mac -

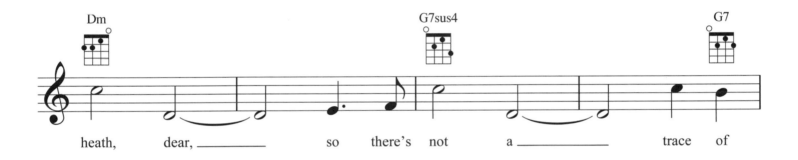

heath,   dear, _____   so there's not a _____ trace of

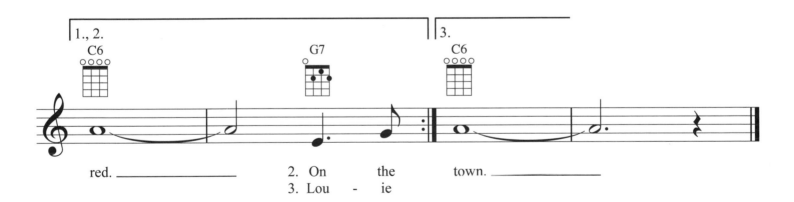

red. _____   2. On the town. _____
      3. Lou - ie

Additional Lyrics

2. On the sidewalk Sunday morning lies a body oozing life.
   Someone's sneaking 'round the corner; is the someone Mack the Knife?
   From a tugboat by the river, a cement bag's dropping down.
   The cement's just for the weight, dear; bet you Mackie's back in town.

3. Louie Miller disappeared, dear, after drawing out his cash.
   And Macheath spends like a sailor; did our boy do something rash?
   Sukey Tawdry, Jenny Diver, Polly Peachum, Lucy Brown.
   Oh, the line forms on the right, dear, now that Mackie's back in town.

Mr. Bojangles

Words and Music by Jerry Jeff Walker

First note

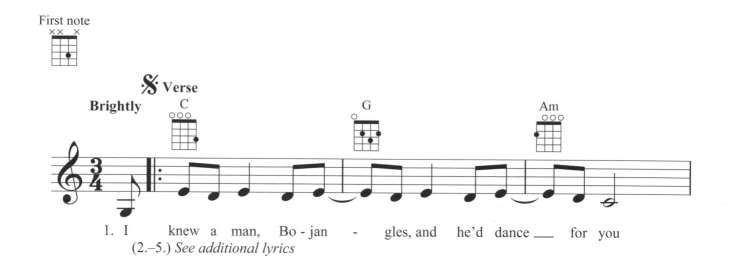

1. I knew a man, Bo - jan - gles, and he'd dance ___ for you
(2.–5.) *See additional lyrics*

in worn - out shoes, with

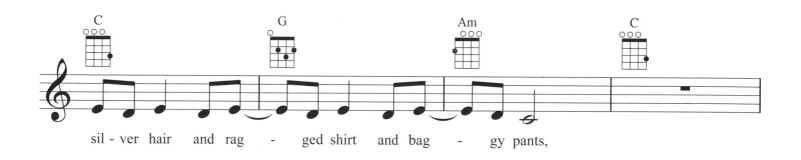

sil - ver hair and rag - ged shirt and bag - gy pants,

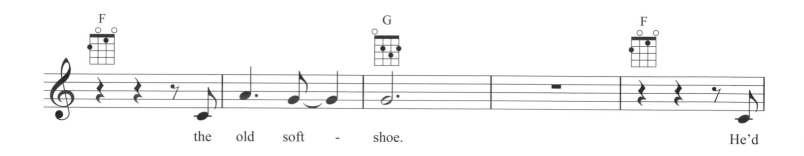

the old soft - shoe. He'd

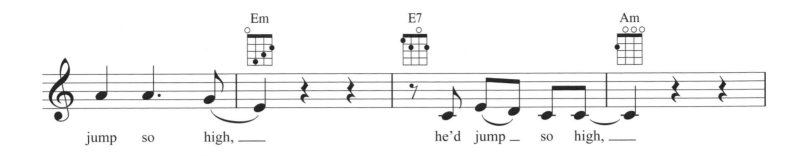

jump   so   high, ____   he'd jump ___ so   high, ____

and   then   he'd   light - ly   touch ___ down. _

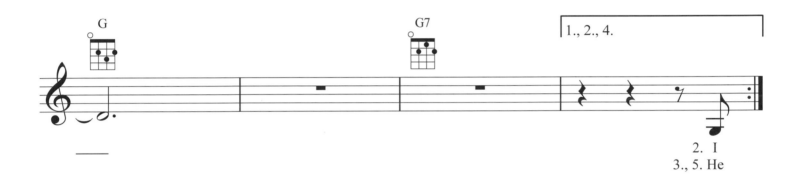

____   2. I
3., 5. He

Mis - ter   Bo   —   jan - gles,

Mis - ter   Bo   —   jan - gles,

Mis - ter Bo - jan - gles,

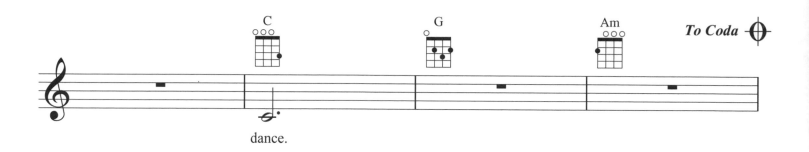

dance.

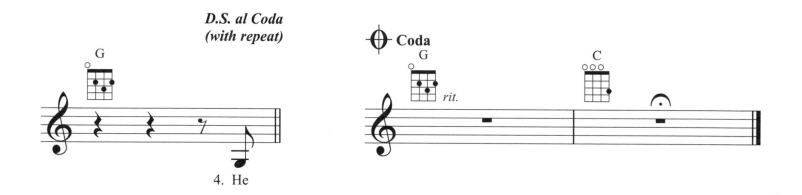

4. He

Additional Lyrics

2. I met him in a cell in New Orleans; I was down and out.
   He looked to me to be the eyes of age as the smoke ran out.
   He talked of life, he talked of life,
   Laughed, clicked his heels and stepped.

3. He said his name, Bojangles, and he danced a lick across the cell.
   He grabbed his pants in feathered stance 'fore he jumped so high,
      and then he clicked his heels.
   He let go a laugh, he let go a laugh,
   Shook back his clothes all around.

4. He danced for those at minstrel shows and county fairs throughout the South.
   He spoke with tears of fifteen years, how his dog and him traveled about.
   The dog up and died, he up and died.
   After twenty years, he still grieves.

5. He said, "I dance now at ev'ry chance in honky-tonks for drinks and tips.
   But most' the time I spend behind these county bars 'cause I drinks a bit."
   He shook his head, and as he shook his head,
   I heard someone ask him: Please, please...

Mr. Tambourine Man

Words and Music by Bob Dylan

First note

Chorus
Moderately

Hey, Mis - ter Tam - bou - rine ___ Man,

play a song ___ for me. ___ I'm not sleep - y and there

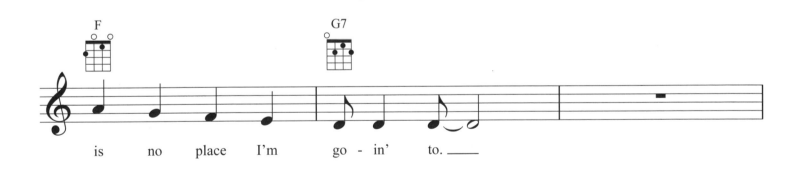

is no place I'm go - in' to. ___

Hey, Mis - ter Tam - bou - rine ___ Man, play a song ___ for me. ___

In the jin - gle jan - gle morn - in', I'll come

fol - low - in' you.

1. Though I
2.–4. *See additional lyrics*

Verse

know that eve - nin's em - pire _____ has re - turned in - to

sand, van - ished from ___ my hand, left me

blind - ly here to stand, but still not sleep - ing.

My wea - ri - ness ___ a - maz - es me, ___ I'm

Additional Lyrics

2. Take me on a trip upon your magic swirlin' ship.
   My senses have been stripped, my hands can't feel to grip.
   My toes too numb to step, wait only for my boot heels to be wanderin'.
   I'm ready to go anywhere, I'm ready for to fade
   Into my own parade, cast your dancin' spell my way.
   I promise to go under it.

3. Though you might hear laughin', spinnin', swingin' madly across the sun,
   It's not aimed at anyone, it's just escapin' on the run.
   And but for the sky, there are no fences facin',
   And if you hear vague traces of skippin' reels of rhyme
   To your tambourine in time, it's just a ragged clown behind.
   I wouldn't pay it any mind; it's just a shadow you're seein' that he's chasin'.

4. Then take me disappearin' through the smoke rings of my mind,
   Down the foggy ruins of time, far past the frozen leaves,
   The haunted, frightened trees out to the windy beach,
   Far from the twisted reach of crazy sorrow,
   Yes, to dance beneath the diamond sky with one hand wavin' free,
   Silhouetted by the sea, circled by the circus sands,
   With all memory and fate driven deep beneath the waves.
   Let me forget about today until tomorrow.

Monday, Monday

Words and Music by John Phillips

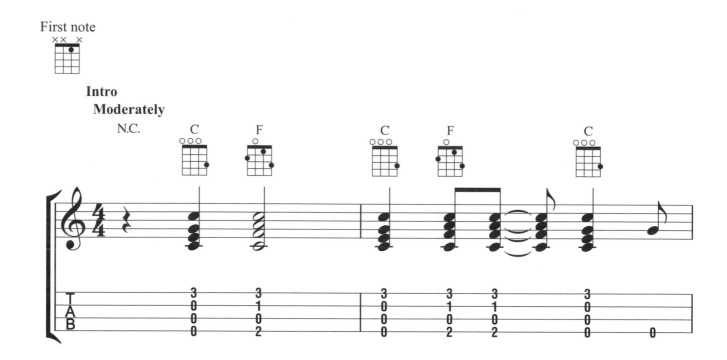

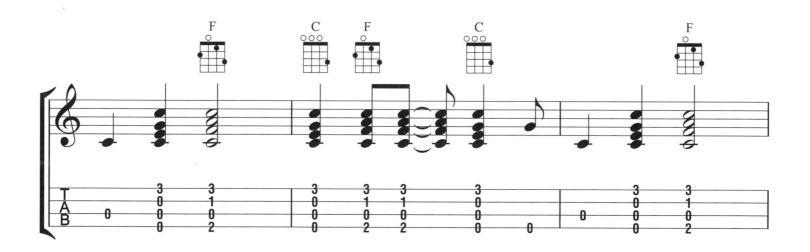

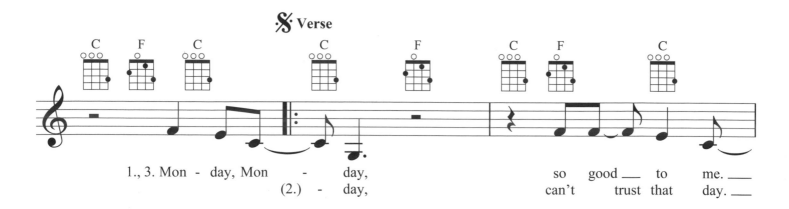

1., 3. Mon - day, Mon - day, so good ___ to me. ___
(2.) - day, can't trust that day. ___

Mon - day morn - in', it was all ___
Mon - day, Mon - day, some - times it

___ I hoped ___ it would be. _____ Oh, Mon - day
just turns out that way. _____ Oh, Mon - day

morn - in', Mon - day morn - in' could - n't guar - an - tee _____
morn - in', you gave me no warn - in' of what was to be. _____

that Mon - day eve - nin' you would still _____ be here ___ with me.
Oh, Mon - day, Mon - day, how could you leave _____ and not take ___ me? ___

1.   2., 3.

___   2. Mon - day, Mon - ___

Bridge

Ev-'ry oth-er day, ___ ev-'ry oth-er day, ev-'ry oth-er day of the week is

fine, yeah! ___ But when-ev-er Mon-day comes,

To Coda

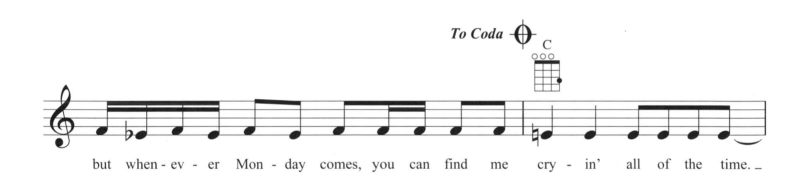

but when-ev-er Mon-day comes, you can find me cry-in' all of the time. _

D.S. al Coda
(Lyric 1, take 2nd ending)

Coda

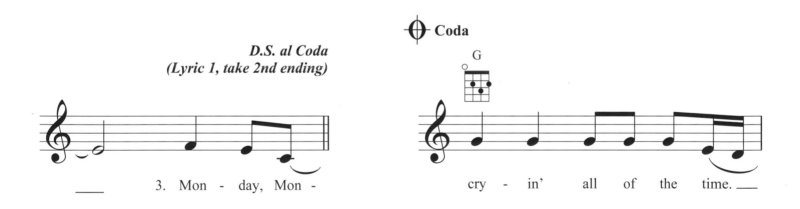

___ 3. Mon-day, Mon-

cry-in' all of the time. ___

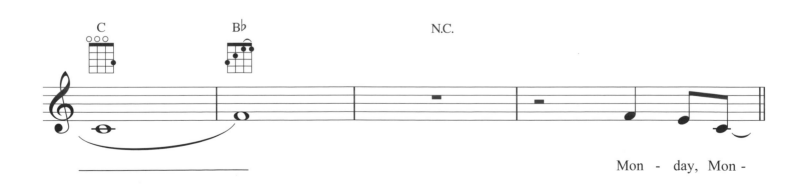

Mon-day, Mon-

Outro-Verse

Over the Rainbow

from THE WIZARD OF OZ
Music by Harold Arlen
Lyric by E.Y. "Yip" Harburg

First note

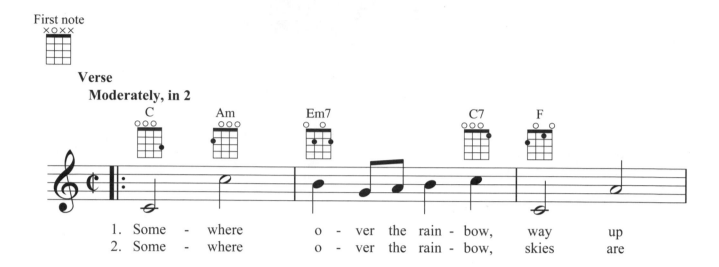

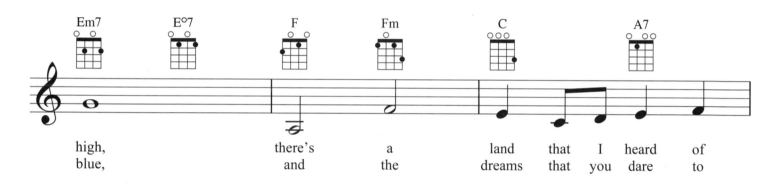

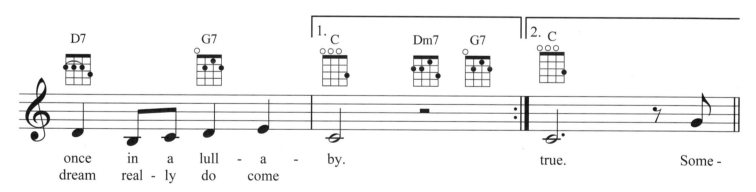

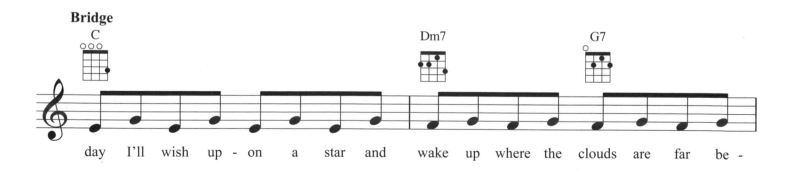

Peaceful Easy Feeling

Words and Music by Jack Tempchin

First note

Verse
Moderately, in 2

1. I like the way ___ your spar - klin' ear - rings ___
2., 3. *See additional lyrics*

lay a - gainst ___ your skin ___ so brown. ___

___ And I wan - na

sleep with you ___ in the des - ert ___ to - night, ___

with a bil - lion stars all a - round. ___

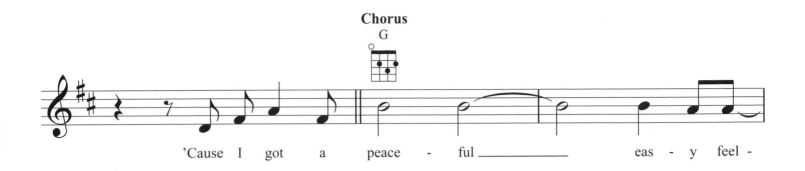

Chorus

'Cause I got a peace - ful _____ eas - y feel -

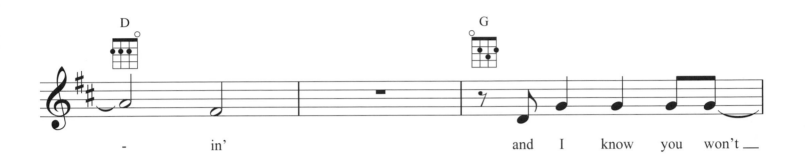

- in' and I know you won't __

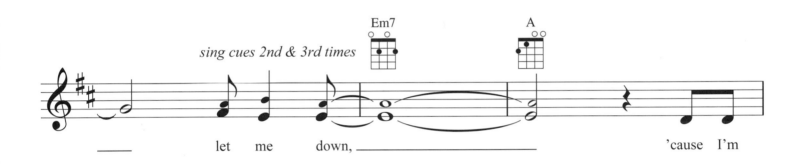

sing cues 2nd & 3rd times

__ let me down, _____ 'cause I'm

To Coda

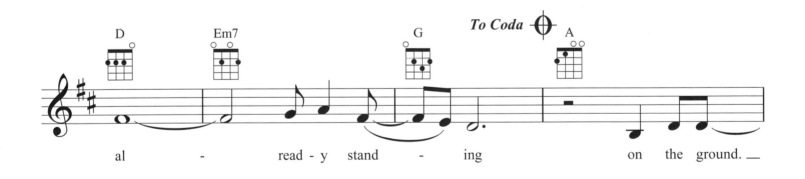

al - read - y stand - ing on the ground. __

2nd time, D.C. al Coda

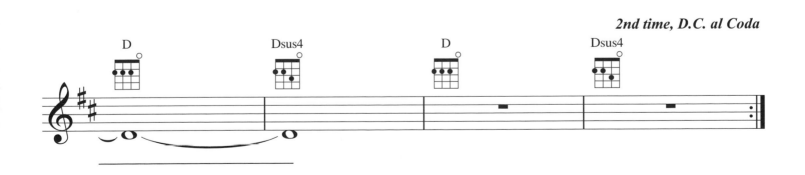

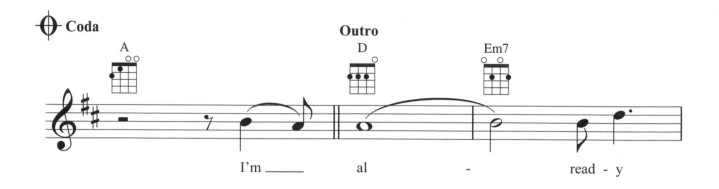

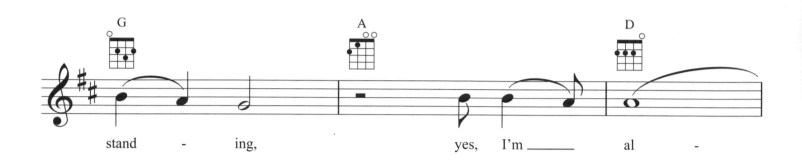

I'm _____ al - read - y

stand - ing, yes, I'm _____ al -

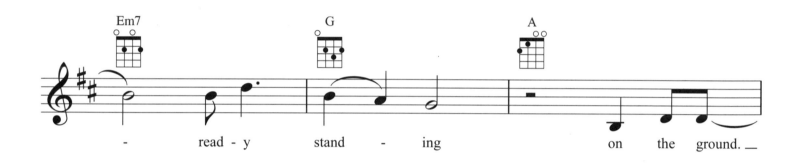

- read - y stand - ing on the ground. __

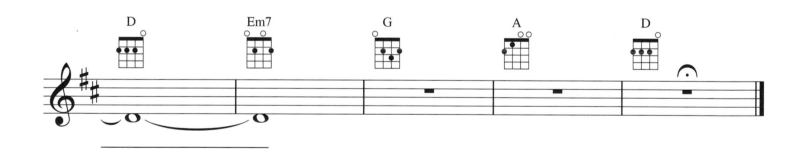

Additional Lyrics

2. And I found out a long time ago
   What a woman can do to your soul.
   Ah, but she can't take you any way
   You don't already know how to go.
   And I got a... *(To Chorus)*

3. I get this feeling I may know you
   As a lover and a friend.
   But this voice keeps whispering in my other ear;
   Tells me I may never see you again.
   'Cause I get a... *(To Chorus)*

One Toke Over the Line

Words and Music by Michael Brewer and Thomas E. Shipley

First note

Chorus
Moderate Country

One toke o - ver the line, ___ sweet Je - sus,)
one toke o - ver the line, ___ sweet Je - sus,)

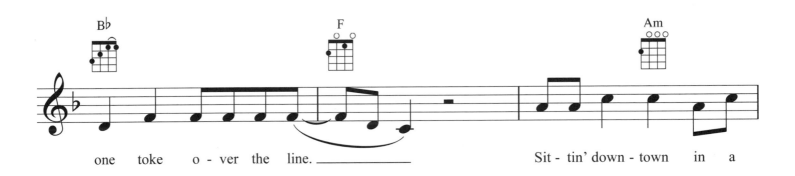

one toke o - ver the line. ___ Sit - tin' down - town in a

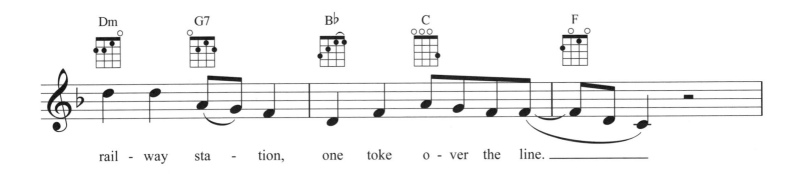

rail - way sta - tion, one toke o - ver the line. ___

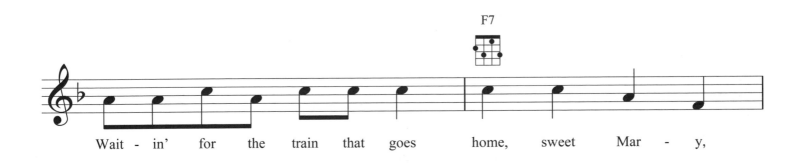

Wait - in' for the train that goes home, sweet Mar - y,

hop - in' that the train is on time. __ Sit - tin' down - town in a

To Coda

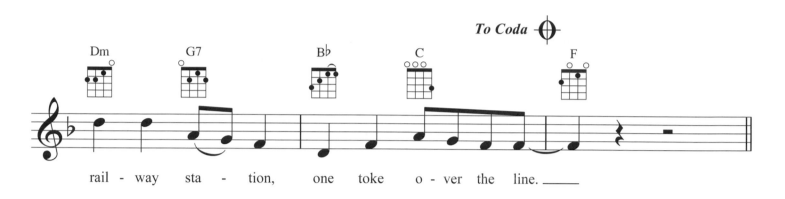

rail - way sta - tion, one toke o - ver the line. _____

Verse

1. Who _____ do you love? _____
2. I _____ sailed a - way _____

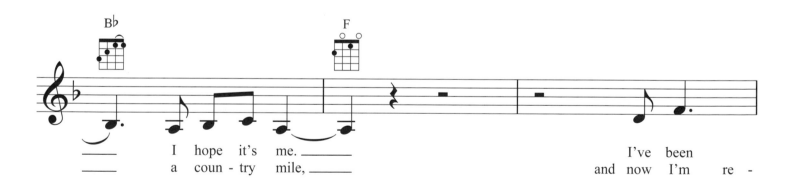

_____ I hope it's me. _____ I've been
_____ a coun - try mile, _____ and now I'm re -

chang - in', as you can plain - ly see. _____
turn - in' and show - in' off my smile. __ I

I felt the joy and I learned a-bout the pain _____
met all the girls and I loved my-self a few, _____

_____ that my ma - ma said. _____
_____ when to my sur - prise, _____

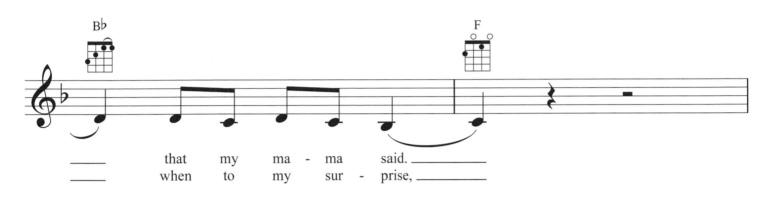

If I should choose to make a part of me, _____
like ev - 'ry - thing else that I've been through, _____

2nd time, D.C. al Coda

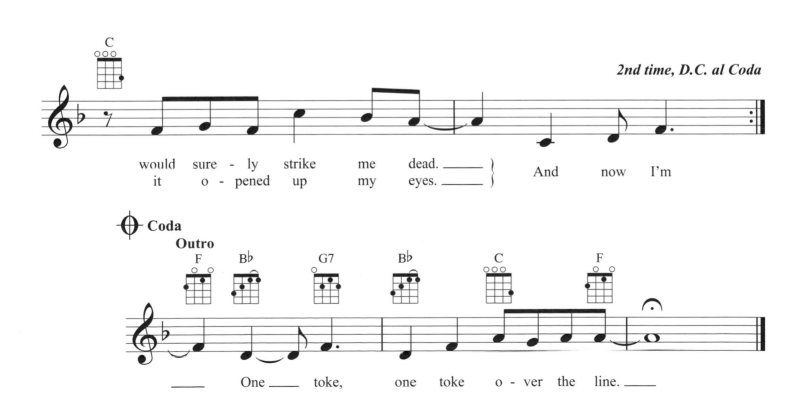

would sure - ly strike me dead. ___
it o - pened up my eyes. ___ } And now I'm

Coda
Outro

_____ One ___ toke, one toke o - ver the line. ___

Pearly Shells

(Pupu 'O 'Ewa)

Words and Music by Webley Edwards and Leon Pober

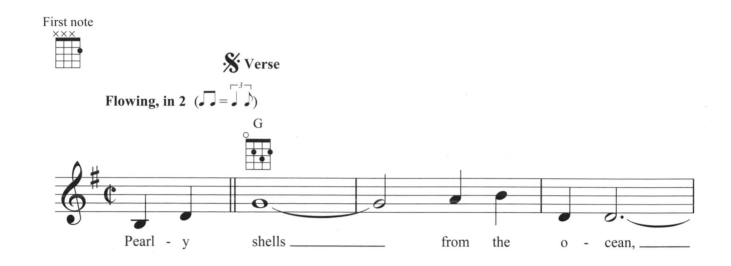

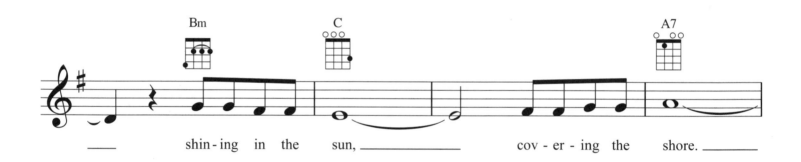

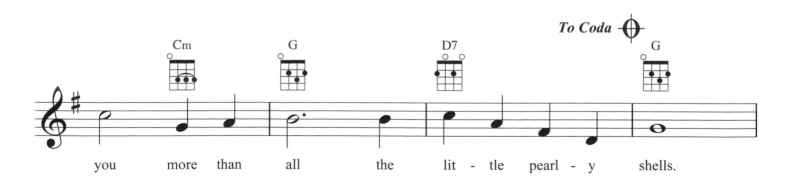

Bridge

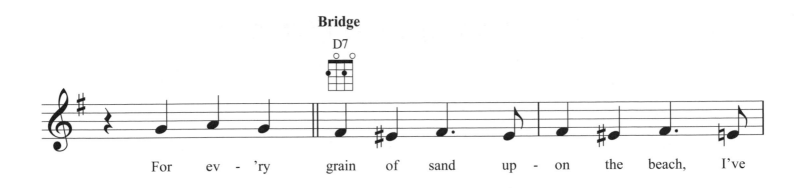

For ev - 'ry grain of sand up - on the beach, I've

got a kiss for you; and I've got more left o - ver

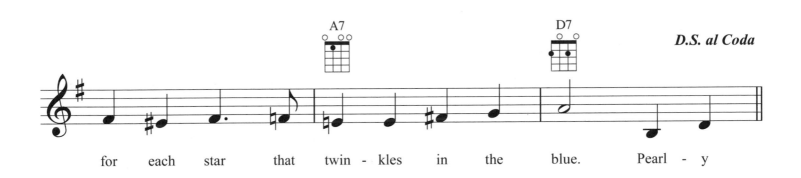

D.S. al Coda

for each star that twin - kles in the blue. Pearl - y

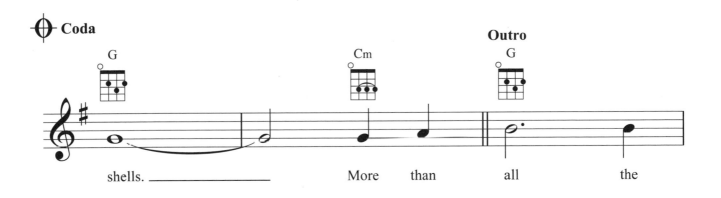

Coda

Outro

shells. _____ More than all the

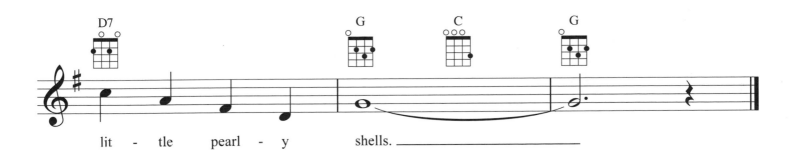

lit - tle pearl - y shells. _____

Puff the Magic Dragon

Words and Music by Lenny Lipton and Peter Yarrow

First note

Verse
Brightly

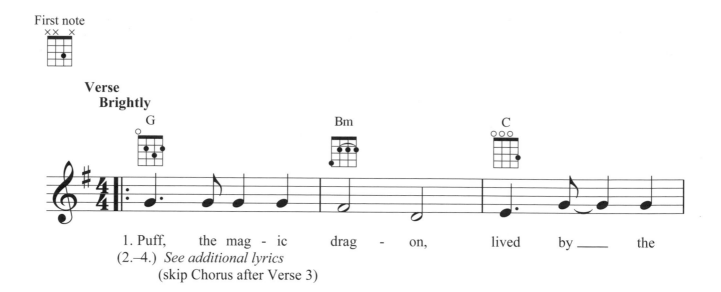

1. Puff,   the mag - ic   drag - on,   lived by ____   the
(2.–4.) *See additional lyrics*
(skip Chorus after Verse 3)

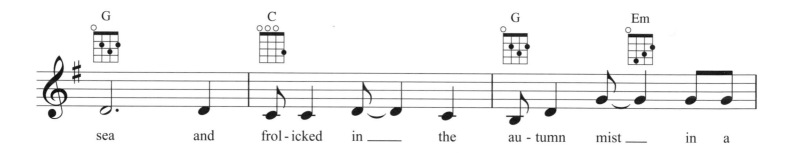

sea   and   frol - icked   in ____   the   au - tumn   mist ____   in a

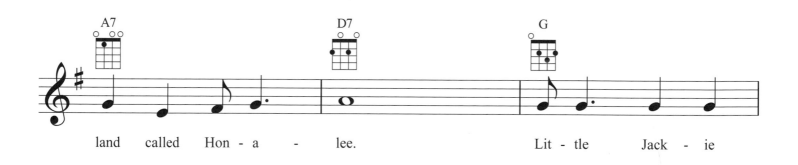

land   called   Hon - a - lee.   Lit - tle   Jack - ie

Pa - per   loved   that   ras - cal   Puff,   and

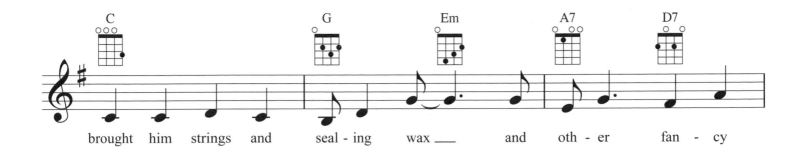

brought him strings and seal - ing wax ___ and oth - er fan - cy

Chorus

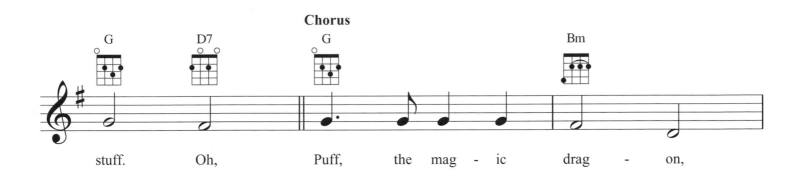

stuff. Oh, Puff, the mag - ic drag - on,

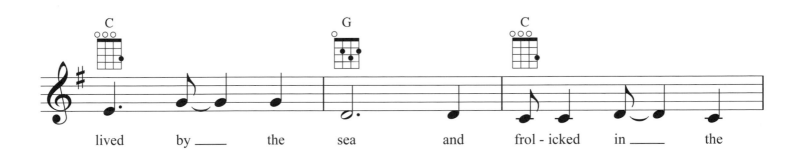

lived by ___ the sea and frol - icked in ___ the

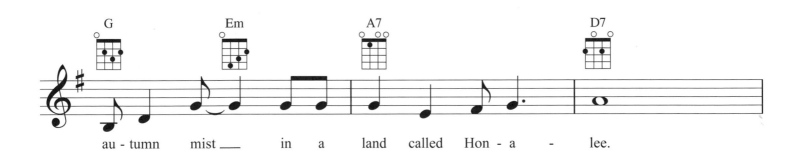

au - tumn mist ___ in a land called Hon - a - lee.

Puff, the mag - ic drag - on, lived by ___ the

sea and frol-icked in ___ the au-tumn mist ___ in a

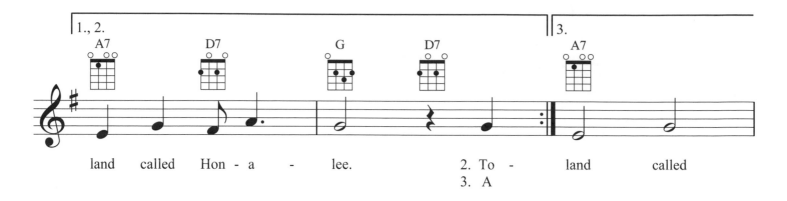

land called Hon - a - lee. 2. To - land called
3. A

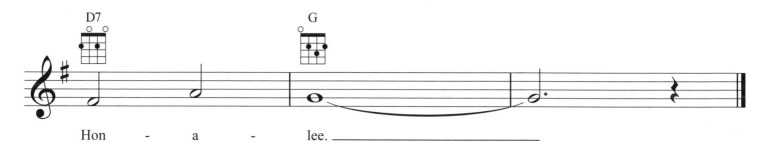

Hon - a - lee. ___

Additional Lyrics

2. Together they would travel on a boat with billowed sail,
   And Jackie kept a lookout perched on Puff's gigantic tail.
   Noble kings and princes would bow whenever they came.
   Pirate ships would lower their flags when Puff roared out his name.

3. A dragon lives forever, but not so little boys.
   Painted wings and giant rings make way for other toys.
   One gray night it happened; Jackie Paper came no more,
   And Puff, that mighty dragon, he ceased his fearless roar. *(To Verse 4)*

4. His head was bent in sorrow, green tears fell like rain.
   Puff no longer went to play along the Cherry Lane.
   Without his lifelong friend, Puff could not be brave.
   So Puff, that mighty dragon, sadly slipped into his cave.

The Rainbow Connection

from THE MUPPET MOVIE
Words and Music by Paul Williams and Kenneth L. Ascher

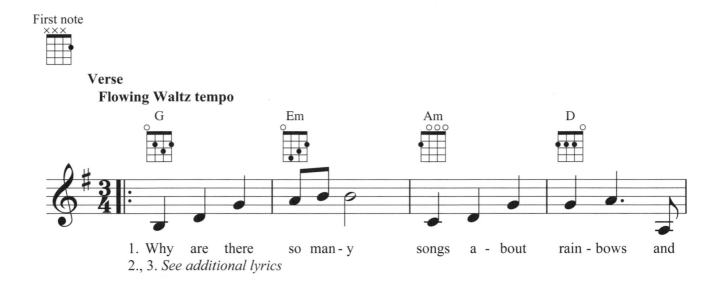

Verse
Flowing Waltz tempo

1. Why are there so man-y songs a-bout rain-bows and
2., 3. *See additional lyrics*

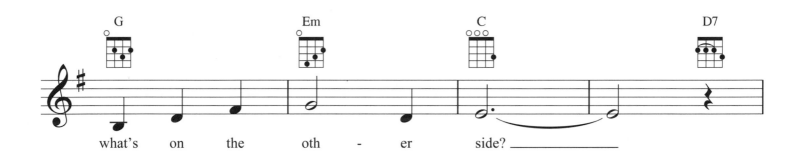

what's on the oth - er side? _____

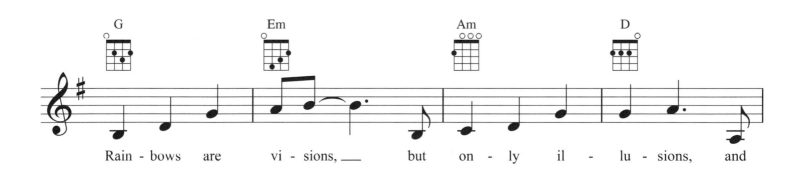

Rain - bows are vi - sions, ___ but on - ly il - lu - sions, and

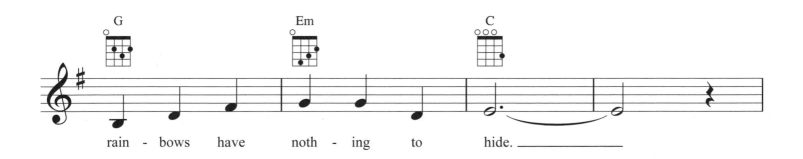

rain - bows have noth - ing to hide. _____

Pre-Chorus

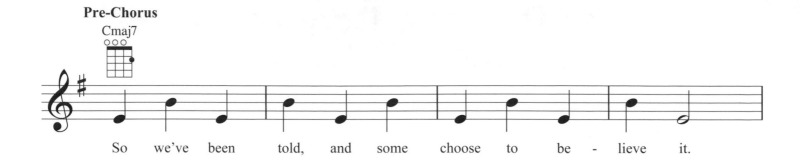

So we've been told, and some choose to be - lieve it.

I know they're wrong; wait and see. _____

Chorus

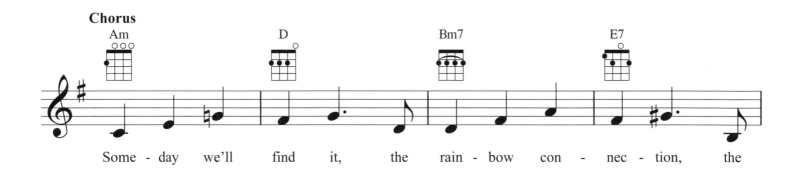

Some - day we'll find it, the rain - bow con - nec - tion, the

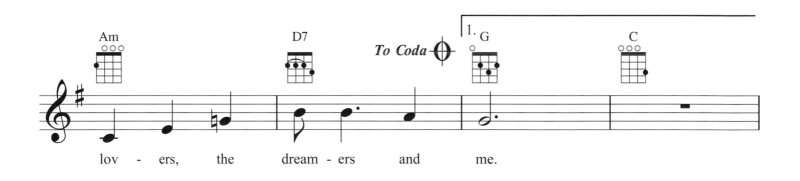

lov - ers, the dream - ers and me.

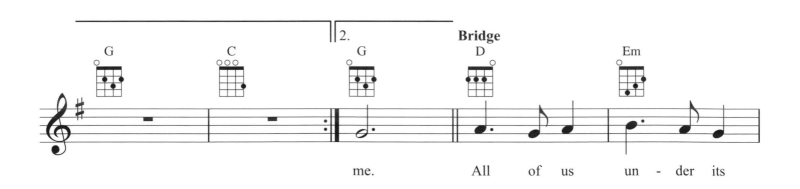

me. All of us un - der its

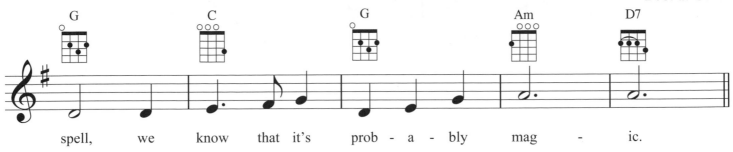

spell,   we   know   that   it's   prob - a - bly   mag -   ic.

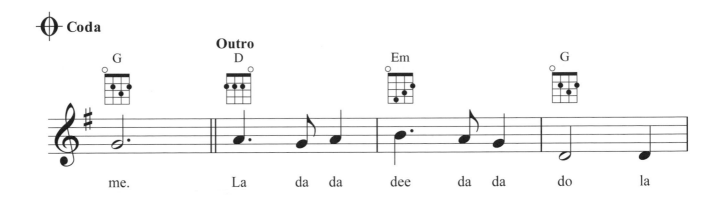

me.   La   da   da   dee   da   da   do   la

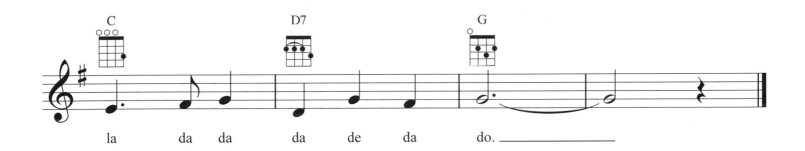

la   da   da   da   de   da   do. _____

Additional Lyrics

2. Who said that ev'ry wish would be heard and answered
   When wished on the morning star?
   Somebody thought of that and someone believed it;
   Look what it's done so far.
   What's so amazing that keeps us stargazing,
   And what do we think we might see?

3. Have you been half asleep and have you heard voices?
   I've heard them calling my name.
   Is this the sweet sound that calls the young sailors?
   The voice might be one and the same.
   I've heard it too many times to ignore it;
   It's something that I'm s'posed to be.

Put a Little Love in Your Heart

Words and Music by Jimmy Holiday, Randy Myers and Jackie DeShannon

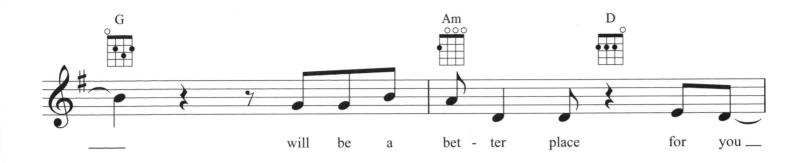

will be a bet - ter place for you

and me. You just wait

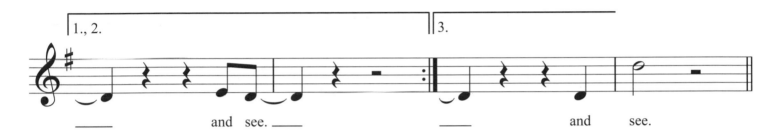

and see. and see.

Outro

Repeat and fade

Put a lit - tle love in your heart.

Additional Lyrics

2. Another day goes by, and still the children cry.
   Put a little love in your heart.
   If you want the world to know we won't let hatred grow,
   Put a little love in your heart.

3. Take a good look around, and if you're lookin' down,
   Put a little love in your heart.
   I hope when you decide, kindness will be your guide.
   Put a little love in your heart.

Raindrops Keep Fallin' on My Head

from BUTCH CASSIDY AND THE SUNDANCE KID
Lyric by Hal David
Music by Burt Bacharach

Rhythm of Love

Words and Music by Tim Lopez

Additional Lyrics

2. Well, my heart beats like a drum,
   A guitar string to the strum,
   A beautiful song to be sung.
   She's got blue eyes, deep like the sea,
   That roll back when she's laughing at me.
   She rises up like the tide the moment her lips meet mine.

D.S. And long after I've gone, you'll still be humming along.
   And I will keep you in my mind, the way you make love so fine.

Stand by Your Man

Words and Music by Tammy Wynette and Billy Sherrill

Keep giv-ing all the love you can.

Stand by your ___ man.

Outro-Chorus

Stand by your man, and show the world ___ you love him. Keep giv-ing all the love you

can. ___ Stand

by your man. ___

Riptide

Words and Music by Vance Joy

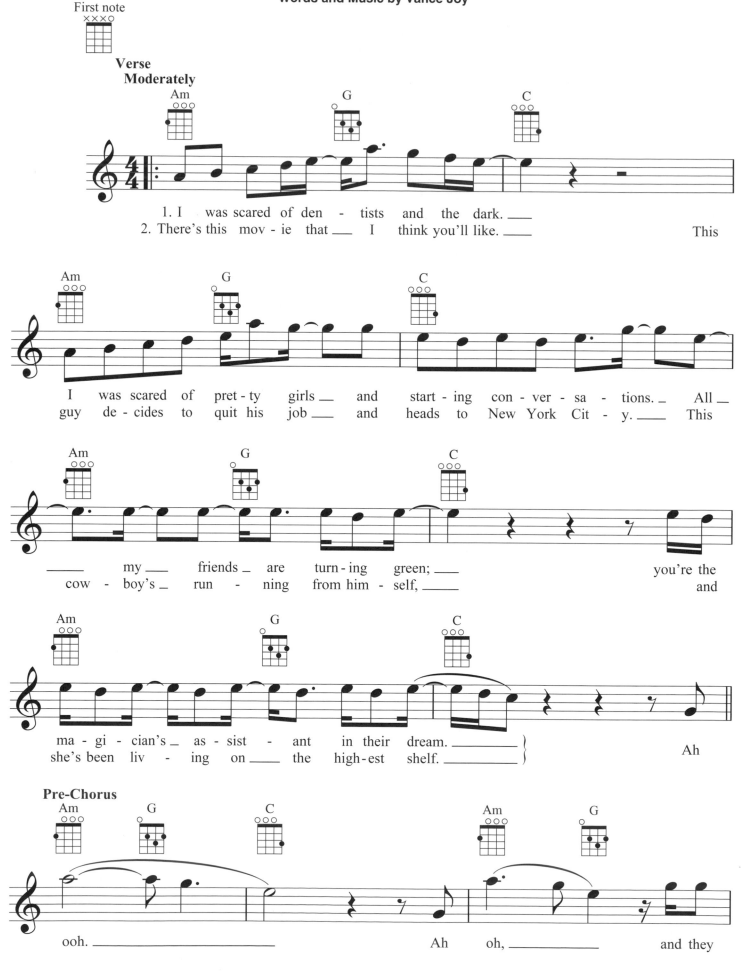

1. I was scared of den - tists and the dark. ___
2. There's this mov - ie that ___ I think you'll like. ___ This

I was scared of pret - ty girls ___ and start - ing con - ver - sa - tions. ___ All ___
guy de - cides to quit his job ___ and heads to New York Cit - y. ___ This

___ my ___ friends ___ are turn - ing green; ___ you're the
cow - boy's ___ run - ning from him - self, ___ and

ma - gi - cian's ___ as - sist - ant in their dream. ___
she's been liv - ing on ___ the high - est shelf. ___ Ah

Pre-Chorus

ooh. ___ Ah oh, ___ and they

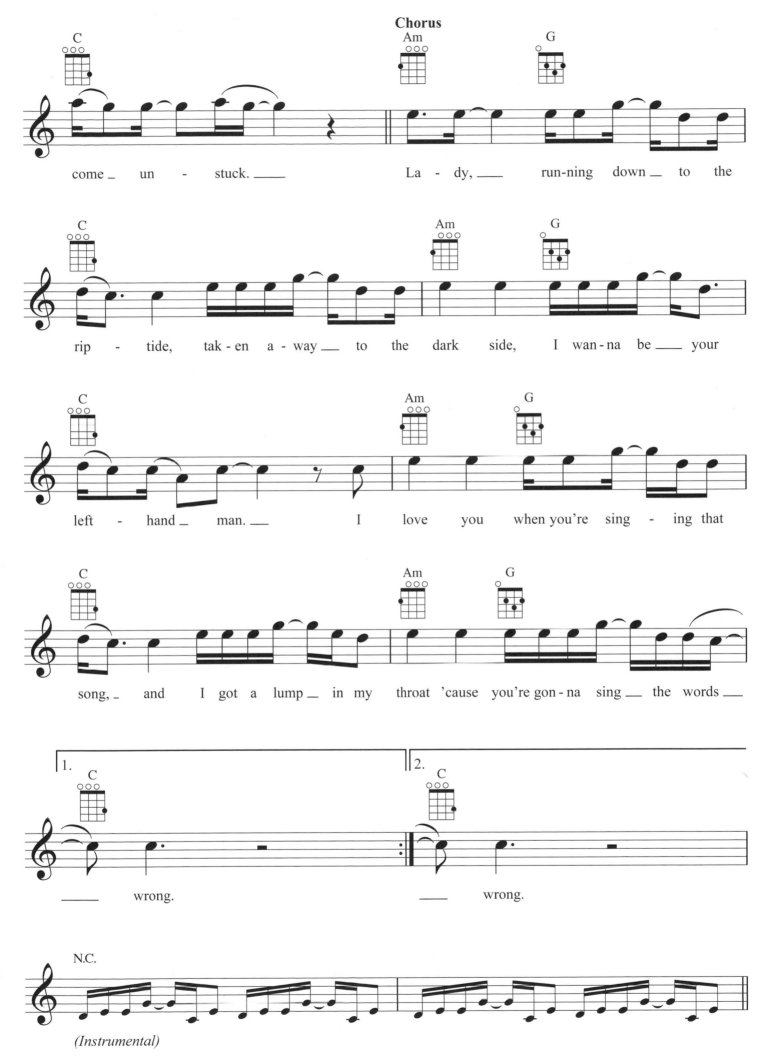

Sing

from SESAME STREET
Words and Music by Joe Raposo

Singin' in the Rain

from SINGIN' IN THE RAIN
Lyric by Arthur Freed
Music by Nacio Herb Brown

read - y for love. Let the storm - y clouds

chase ev - 'ry - one _____ from the place. Come

on _____ with the rain; I've a smile _____ on my

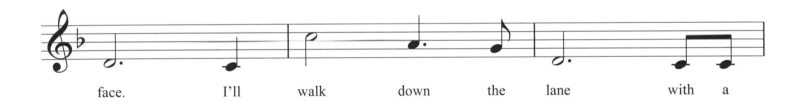

face. I'll walk down the lane with a

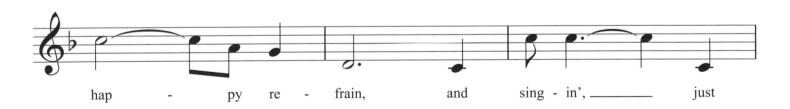

hap - py re - frain, and sing - in', _____ just

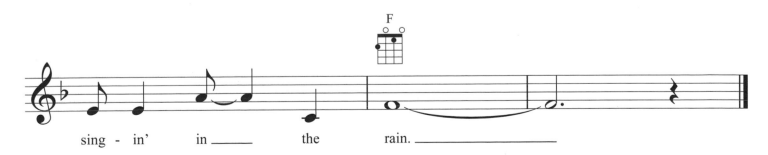

sing - in' in _____ the rain. _____

Sweet Caroline

Words and Music by Neil Diamond

Interlude

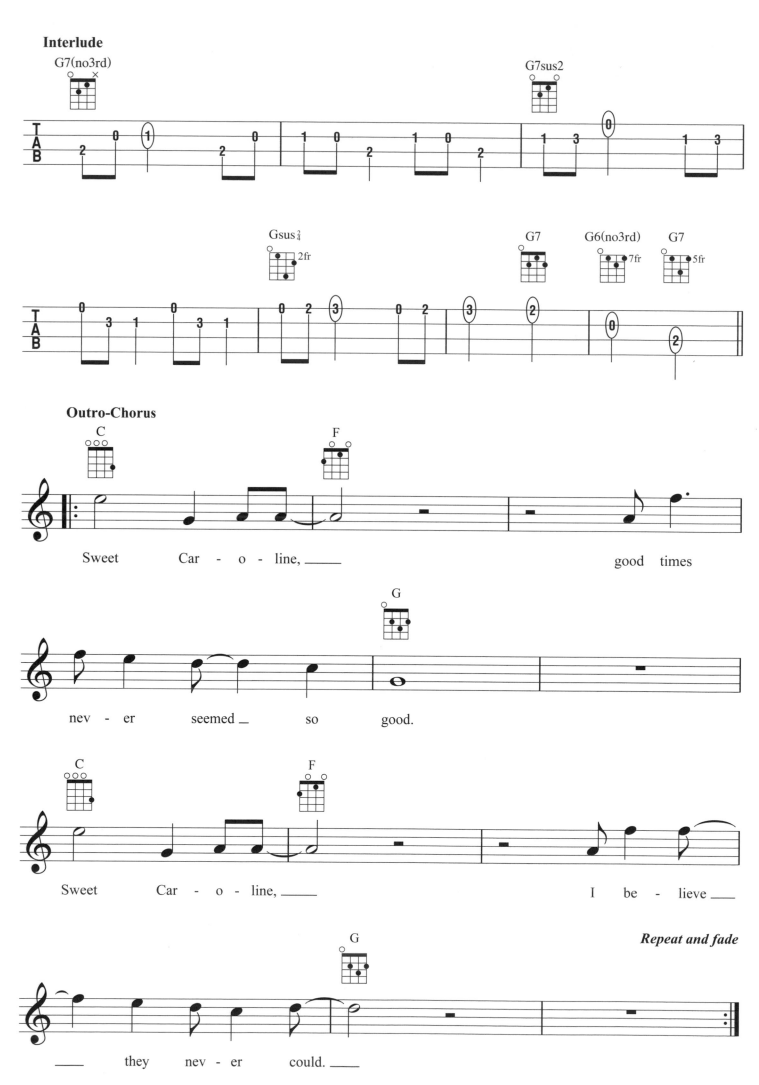

Outro-Chorus

Sweet Car - o - line, _____ good times

nev - er seemed _ so good.

Sweet Car - o - line, _____ I be - lieve _____

Repeat and fade

_____ they nev - er could. _____

Take Me Home, Country Roads

Words and Music by John Denver, Bill Danoff and Taffy Nivert

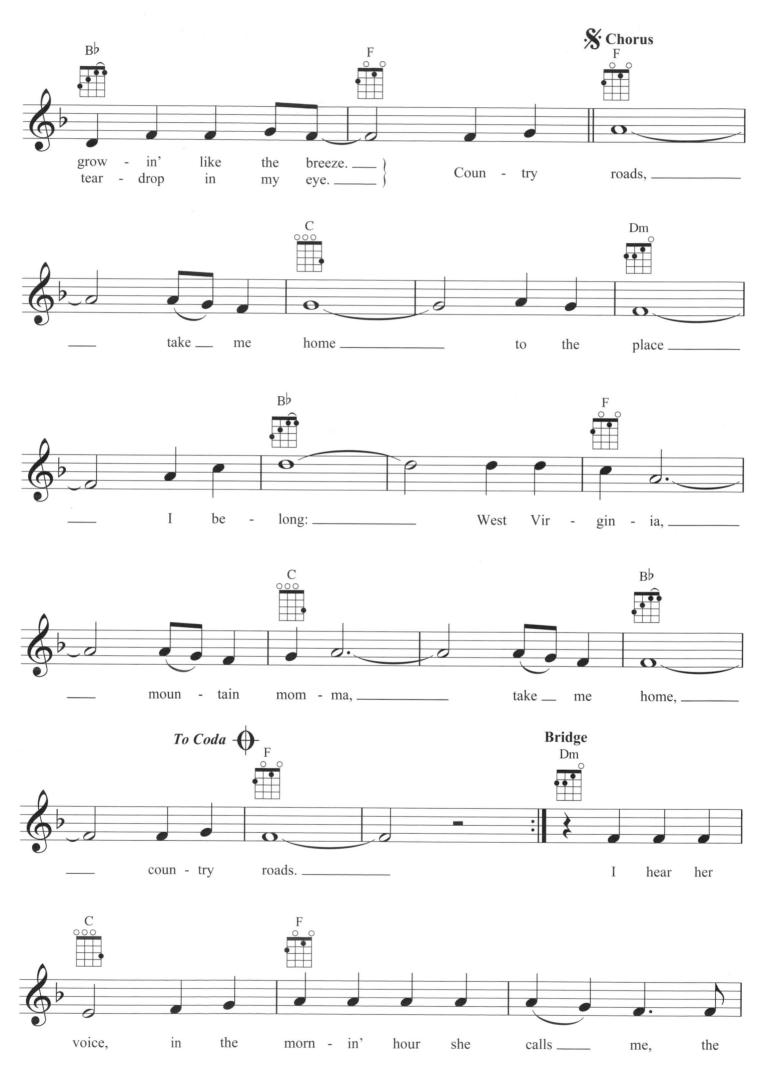

grow - in' like the breeze. ——
tear - drop in my eye. ——

Coun - try roads, ——

—— take —— me home —— to the place ——

—— I be - long: —— West Vir - gin - ia, ——

—— moun - tain mom - ma, —— take —— me home, ——

To Coda ⊕

—— coun - try roads. ——

Bridge

I hear her

voice, in the morn - in' hour she calls —— me, the

That's Amoré

(That's Love)

from the Paramount Picture THE CADDY
Words by Jack Brooks
Music by Harry Warren

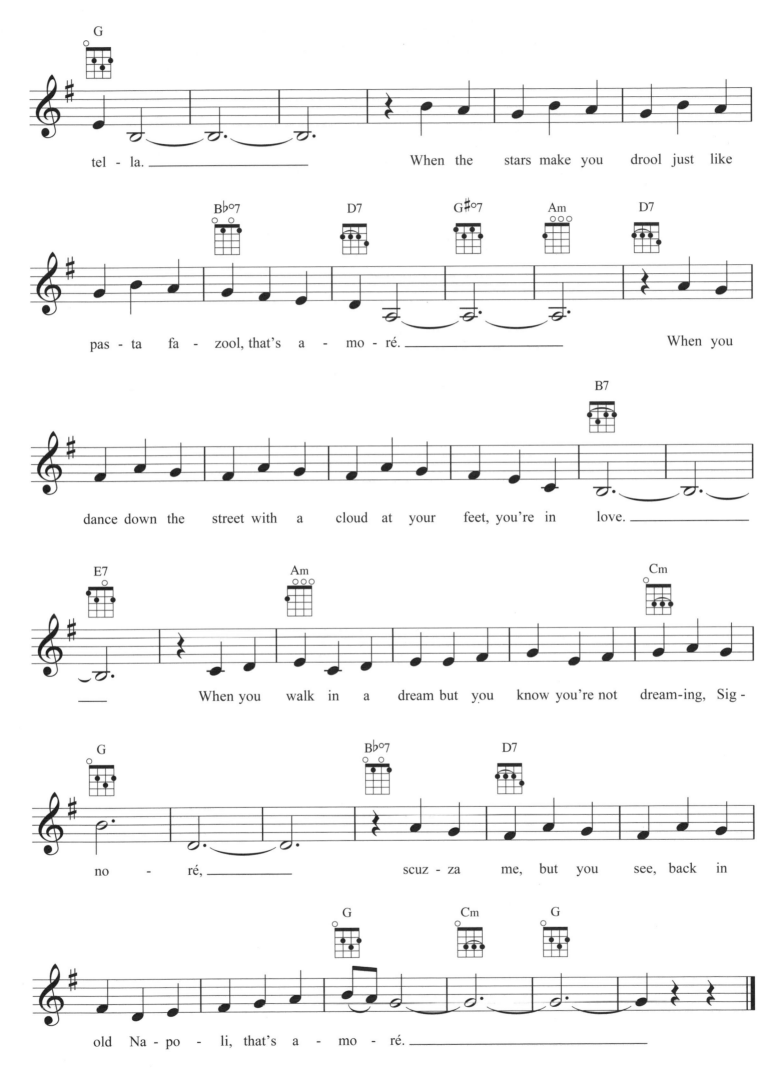

tel - la. _____ When the stars make you drool just like

pas - ta fa - zool, that's a - mo - ré. _____ When you

dance down the street with a cloud at your feet, you're in love. _____

When you walk in a dream but you know you're not dream-ing, Sig-

no - ré, _____ scuz - za me, but you see, back in

old Na - po - li, that's a - mo - ré. _____

This Land Is Your Land

Words and Music by Woody Guthrie

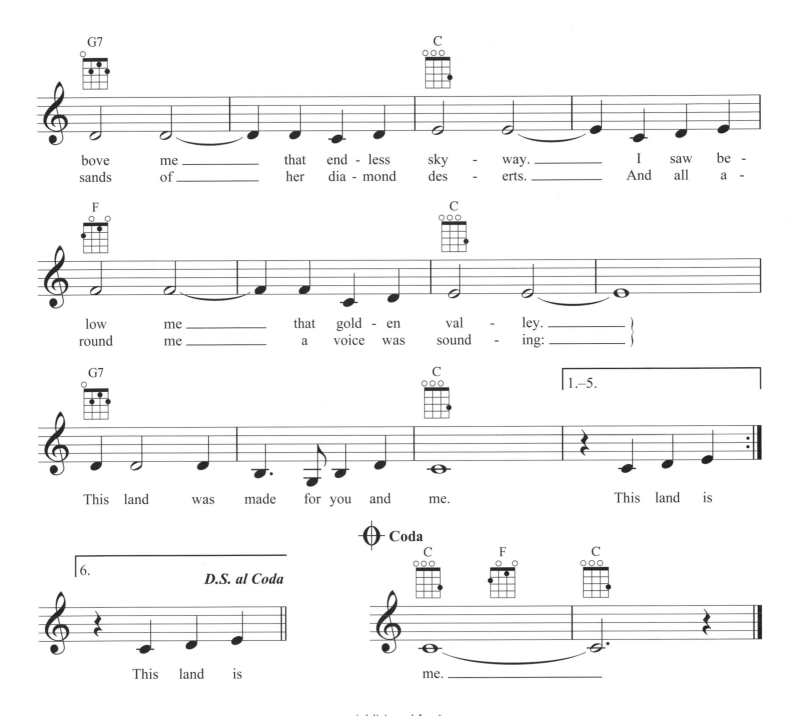

Additional Lyrics

3. When the sun came shining, and I was strolling,
   And the wheat fields waving, and the dust clouds rolling,
   As the fog was lifting, a voice was chanting:
   This land was made for you and me.

4. As I went walking, I saw a sign there,
   And on the sign it said, "No Trespassing,"
   But on the other side it didn't say nothing;
   That side was made for you and me.

5. In the shadow of the steeple, I saw my people.
   By the relief office, I saw my people.
   As they stood there hungry, I stood there asking:
   Is this land made for you and me?

6. Nobody living can ever stop me
   As I go walking that freedom highway.
   Nobody living can ever make me turn back;
   This land was made for you and me.

Top of the World

Words and Music by John Bettis and Richard Carpenter

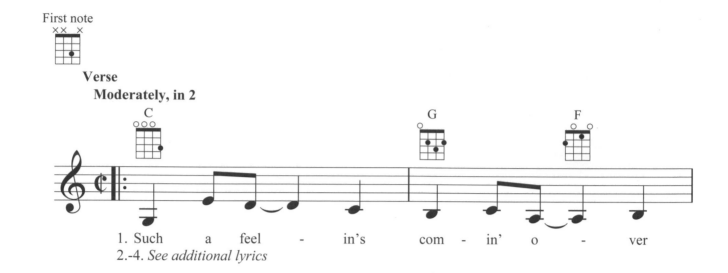

First note

Verse
Moderately, in 2

1. Such a feel - in's com - in' o - ver
2.-4. *See additional lyrics*

me, ___ there is won - der in ___ most

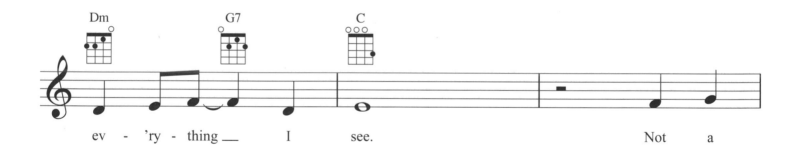

ev - 'ry - thing ___ I see. Not a

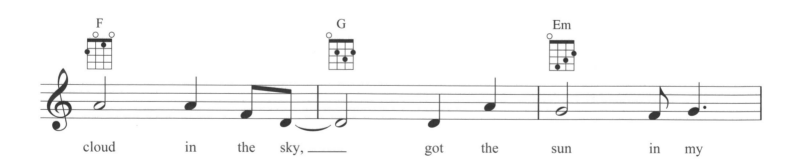

cloud in the sky, ___ got the sun in my

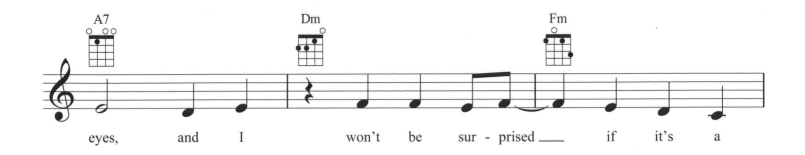

eyes,   and I   won't be sur - prised ___ if it's a

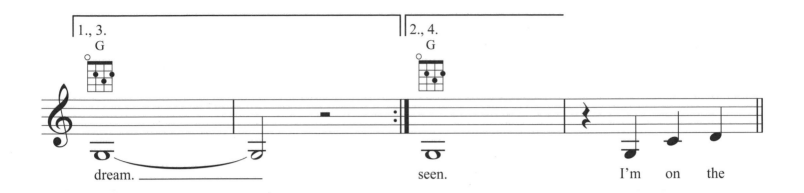

dream. _____   seen.   I'm on the

Chorus

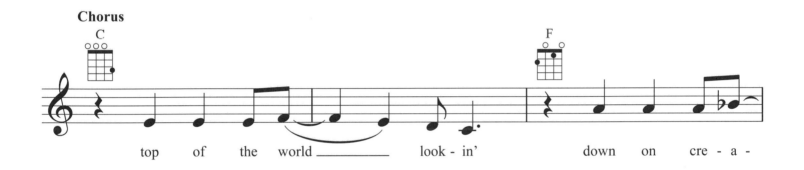

top of the world _____ look - in'   down on cre - a -

- tion, and the on - ly ex - pla - na - tion I ____ can ___

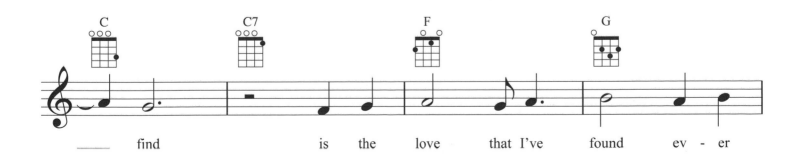

___ find   is the love that I've found ev - er

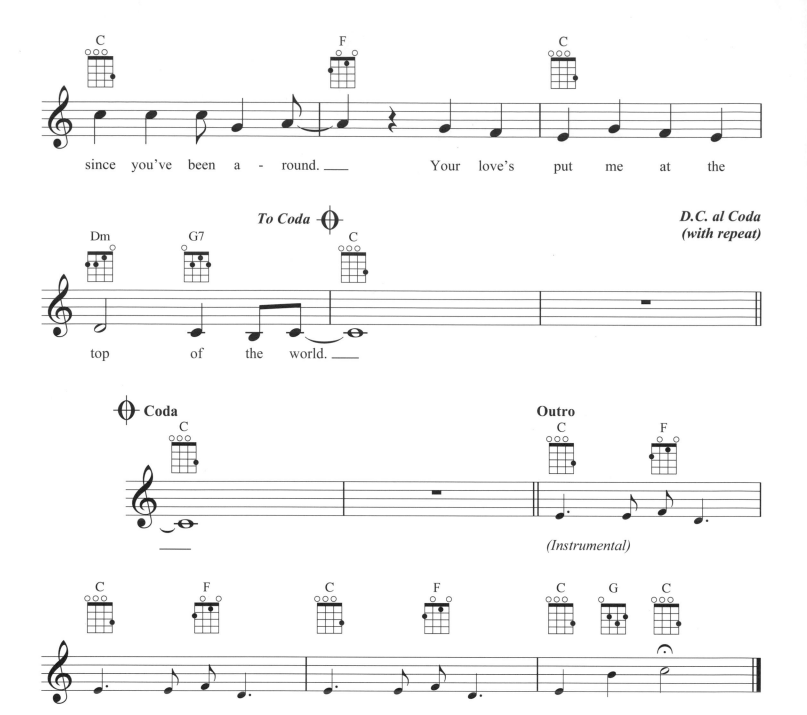

since you've been a - round. ___ Your love's put me at the

top of the world. ___

To Coda ⊕

D.C. al Coda **(with repeat)**

⊕ **Coda**

Outro

(Instrumental)

Additional Lyrics

2. Everything I want the world to be
   Is now coming true especially for me.
   And the reason is clear; it's because you are here.
   You're the nearest thing to heaven that I've seen.

3. Something in the wind has learned my name,
   And it's telling me that things are not the same.
   In the leaves on the trees and the touch of the breeze,
   There's a pleasing sense of happiness for me.

4. There is only one wish on my mind:
   When this day is through, I hope that I will find
   That tomorrow will be just the same for you and me.
   All I need will be mine if you are here.

We Are the World

Words and Music by Lionel Richie and Michael Jackson

1. There comes a time ___ when we heed a cer - tain call, ___
2., 3. *See additional lyrics*

___ when the world must come to - geth - er as

one. There are peo - ple dy - ing,

oh, and it's time ___ to lend a hand to life, ___

___ the great - est gift ___ of all.

Additional Lyrics

2. We can't go on pretending day by day
   That someone, somewhere will soon make a change.
   We are all a part of God's great big family,
   And the truth, you know: love is all we need.

3. Send them your heart so they know that someone cares,
   And their lives will be stronger and free.
   As God has shown us by turning stone to bread,
   And so we all must lend a helping hand.

We'll Sing in the Sunshine

Words and Music by Gale Garnett

First note

We'll sing in the sun - shine, ____ we'll laugh ev - 'ry

day; _____ we'll sing in the sun - shine ____

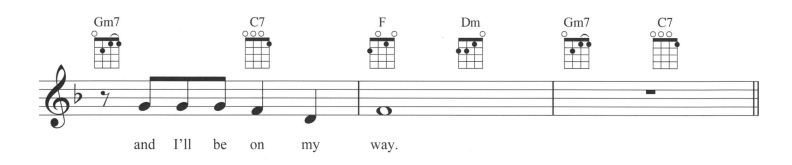

and I'll be on my way.

Verse

1. I will nev - er love ____ you; ____ the cost of love's too dear. ____
2. sing to you each morn - ing, ____ I'll kiss you ev - 'ry night. ____
3. dad - dy, he once told ____ me: ____ don't love you an - y man, ____
4. when our year has end - ed ____ and I have gone a - way, ____

What a Wonderful World

Words and Music by George David Weiss and Bob Thiele

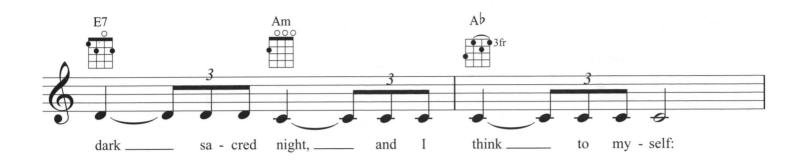

dark _____ sa - cred night, _____ and I think _____ to my - self:

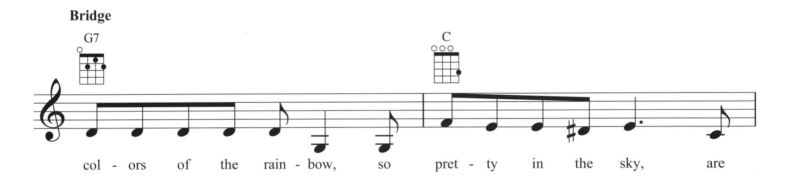

What a won - der - ful world. _____ The

Bridge

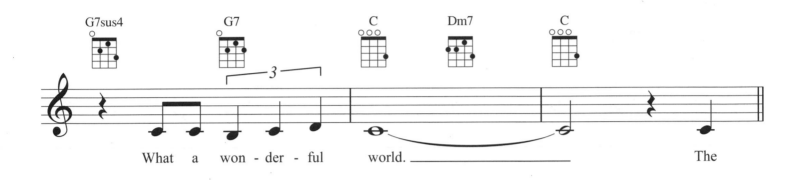

col - ors of the rain - bow, so pret - ty in the sky, are

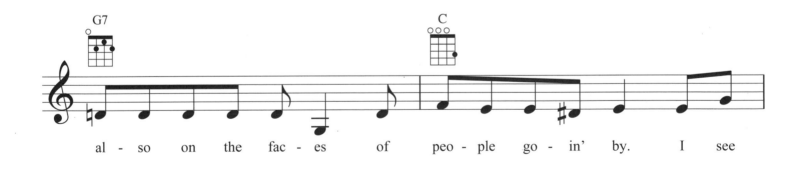

al - so on the fac - es of peo - ple go - in' by. I see

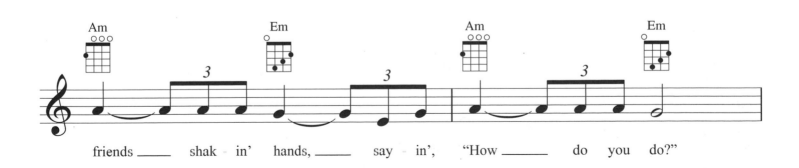

friends _____ shak - in' hands, _____ say - in', "How _____ do you do?"

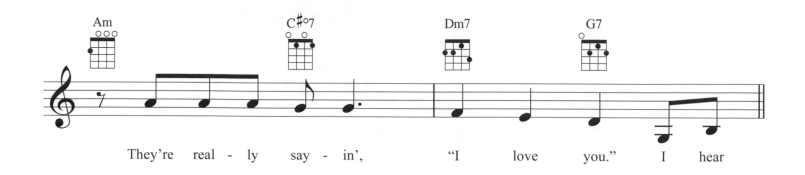

They're real - ly say - in', "I love you." I hear

Outro-Verse

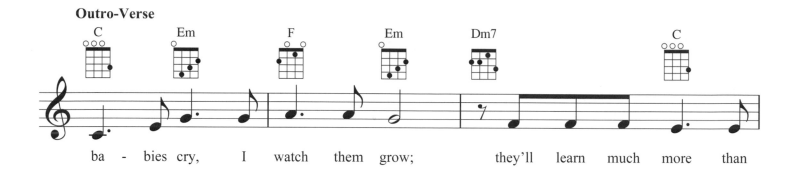

ba - bies cry, I watch them grow; they'll learn much more than

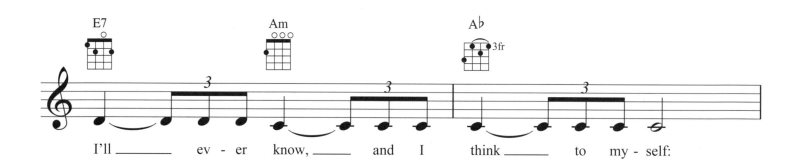

I'll _____ ev - er know, _____ and I think _____ to my - self:

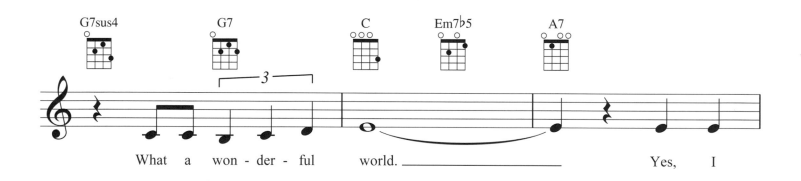

What a won - der - ful world. _____ Yes, I

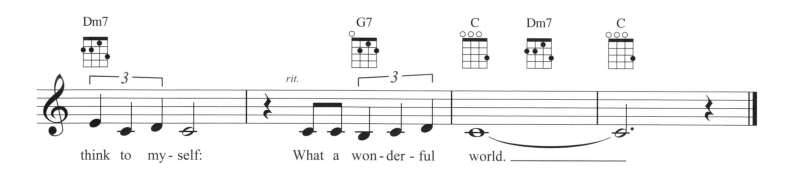

think to my - self: What a won - der - ful world. _____

When I'm Sixty-Four

Words and Music by John Lennon and Paul McCartney

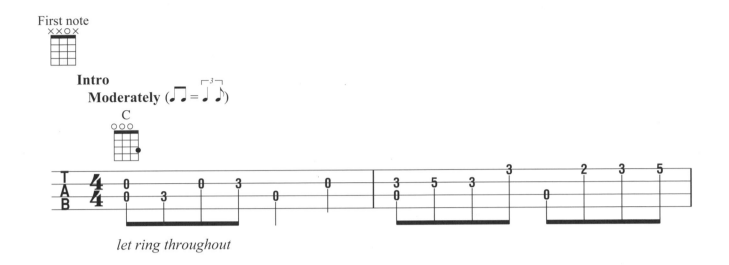

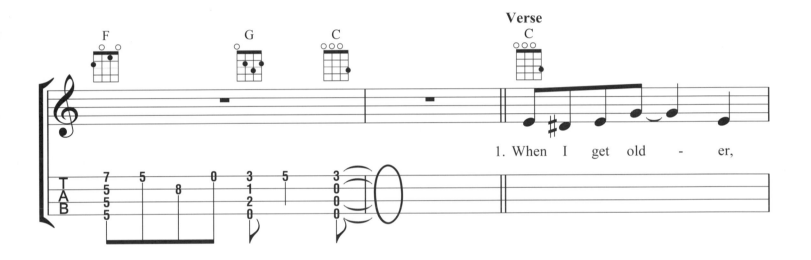

1. When I get old - er,

los - ing my hair, __ man - y years from now, __

will you still be send - ing me a val - en - tine, __ birth - day greet - ings,

bot - tle of wine? __   If I'd been out __ till   quar - ter to three, __

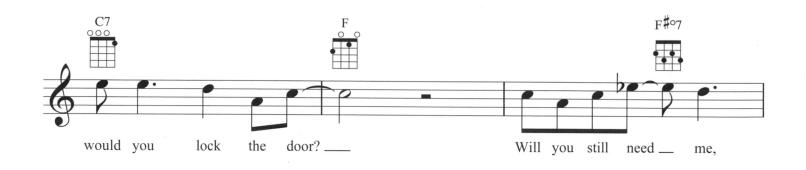

would you   lock   the door? __   Will you still need __ me,

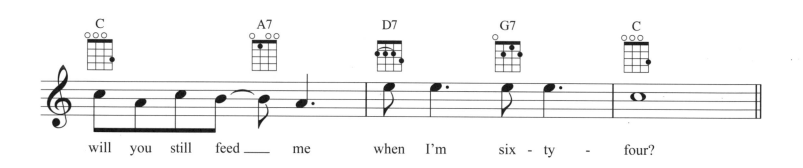

will   you   still   feed ___ me   when   I'm   six - ty - four?

Bridge

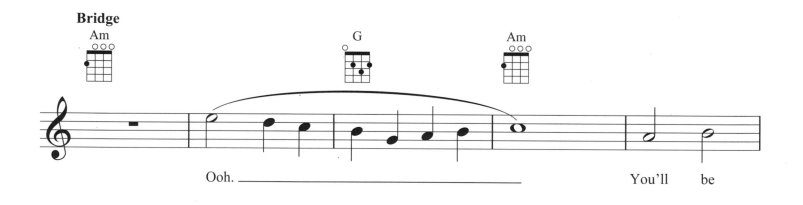

Ooh. ____   You'll   be

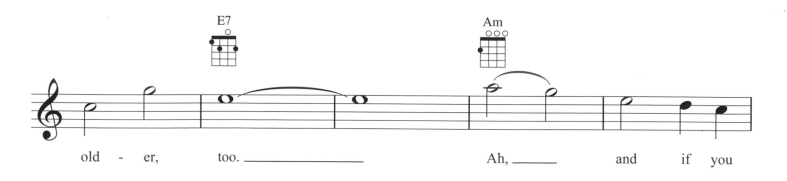

old - er,   too. ____   Ah, ____   and   if you

say the word, _____ I could stay with

you.

§ **Verse**

2. I could be hand - y mend - ing a fuse _____ when your lights have gone. _____
3. Send me a post - card, drop me a line _____ stat - ing point of view. _____

_____ You can knit a sweat - er by the fire - side; _____
_____ In - di - cate pre - cise - ly what you mean to say, _____

Sun - day morn - ing, go for a ride. _____ Do - ing the gar - den,
yours sin - cere - ly wast - ing a - way. _____ Give me your an - swer,

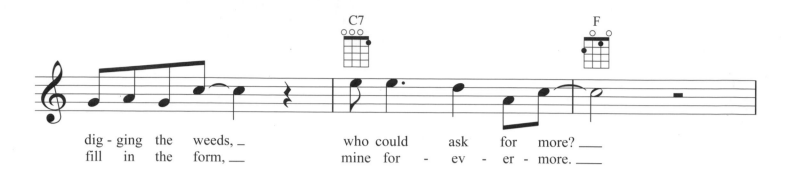

dig - ging the weeds, __ who could ask for more? __
fill in the form, __ mine for - ev - er - more. __

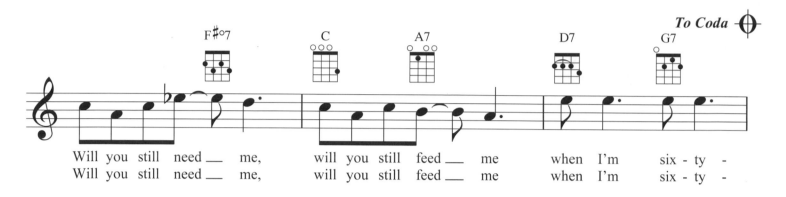

To Coda

Will you still need __ me, will you still feed __ me when I'm six - ty -
Will you still need __ me, will you still feed __ me when I'm six - ty -

Bridge

four? Ev - 'ry sum - mer we can rent a cot - tage in the Isle of Wight __

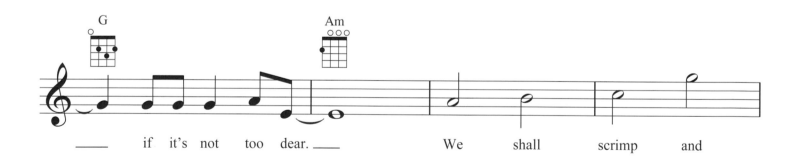

__ if it's not too dear. __ We shall scrimp and

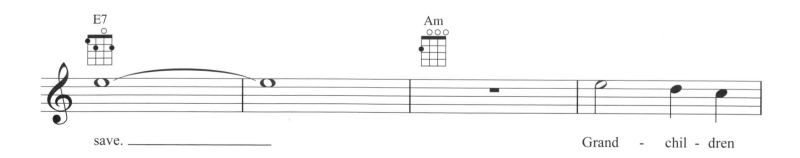

save. _____ Grand - chil - dren

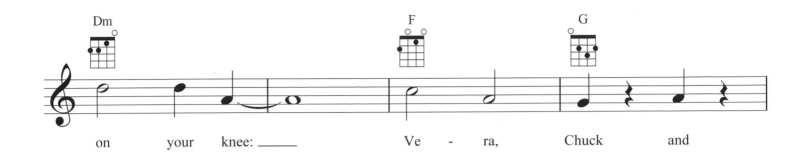

on your knee: _____ Ve - ra, Chuck and

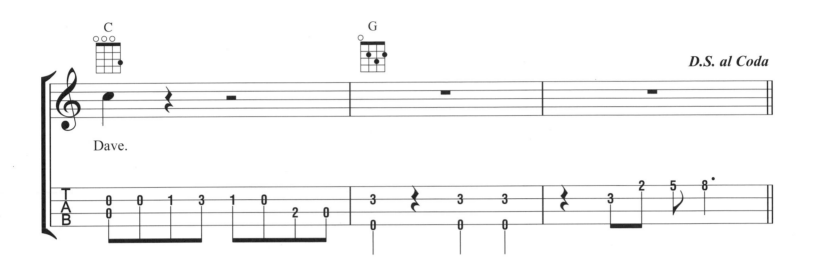

D.S. al Coda

Dave.

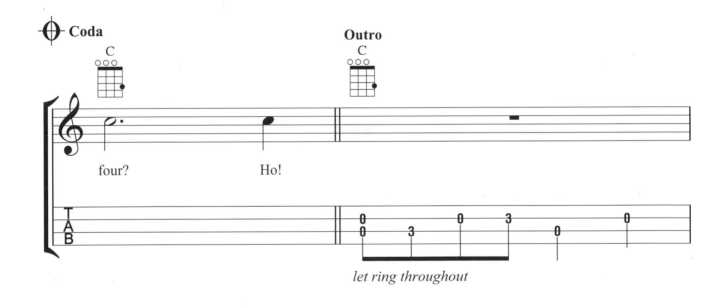

Coda

Outro

four? Ho!

let ring throughout

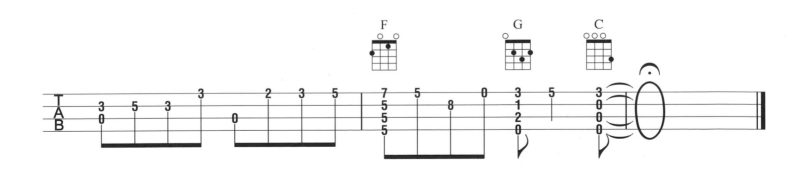

You Are My Sunshine

Words and Music by Jimmie Davis

my on - ly sun - shine, _____ you make me

hap - py _____ when skies are gray. _____

_____ You'll nev - er know, dear, _____ how much I

love you. _____ Please don't take my sun - shine a -

1., 2.

3.

way. _____ 2. I'll al - ways   way. _____
         3. You told me

Additional Lyrics

2. I'll always love you and make you happy
   If you will only say the same.
   But if you leave me to love another,
   You'll regret it all someday.

3. You told me once, dear, you really loved me
   And no one else could come between.
   But now you've left me and love another;
   You have shattered all my dreams.

UKULELE CHORD SONGBOOKS

This series features convenient 6" x 9" books with complete lyrics and chord symbols for dozens of great songs. Each song also includes chord grids at the top of every page and the first notes of the melody for easy reference.

ACOUSTIC ROCK

60 tunes: American Pie • Band on the Run • Catch the Wind • Daydream • Every Rose Has Its Thorn • Hallelujah • Iris • More Than Words • Patience • The Sound of Silence • Space Oddity • Sweet Talkin' Woman • Wake up Little Susie • Who'll Stop the Rain • and more.
00702482 . . . . $15.99

THE BEATLES

100 favorites: Across the Universe • Carry That Weight • Dear Prudence • Good Day Sunshine • Here Comes the Sun • If I Fell • Love Me Do • Michelle • Ob-La-Di, Ob-La-Da • Revolution • Something • Ticket to Ride • We Can Work It Out • and many more.
00703065 . . . . $22.99

BEST SONGS EVER

70 songs: All I Ask of You • Bewitched • Edelweiss • Just the Way You Are • Let It Be • Memory • Moon River • Over the Rainbow • Someone to Watch over Me • Unchained Melody • You Are the Sunshine of My Life • You Raise Me Up • and more.
00117050 . . . . $16.99

CHILDREN'S SONGS

80 classics: Alphabet Song • "C" Is for Cookie • Do-Re-Mi • I'm Popeye the Sailor Man • Mickey Mouse March • Oh! Susanna • Polly Wolly Doodle • Puff the Magic Dragon • The Rainbow Connection • Sing • Three Little Fishies (Itty Bitty Poo) • and many more.
00702473 . . . . $17.99

CHRISTMAS CAROLS

75 favorites: Away in a Manger • Coventry Carol • The First Noel • Good King Wenceslas • Hark! the Herald Angels Sing • I Saw Three Ships • Joy to the World • O Little Town of Bethlehem • Still, Still, Still • Up on the Housetop • What Child Is This? • and more.
00702474 . . . . $14.99

CHRISTMAS SONGS

55 Christmas classics: Do They Know It's Christmas? • Frosty the Snow Man • Happy Xmas (War Is Over) • Jingle-Bell Rock • Little Saint Nick • The Most Wonderful Time of the Year • White Christmas • and more.
00101776 . . . . $14.99

ISLAND SONGS

60 beach party tunes: Blue Hawaii • Day-O (The Banana Boat Song) • Don't Worry, Be Happy • Island Girl • Kokomo • Lovely Hula Girl • Mele Kalikimaka • Red, Red Wine • Surfer Girl • Tiny Bubbles • Ukulele Lady • and many more.
00702471 . . . . $16.99

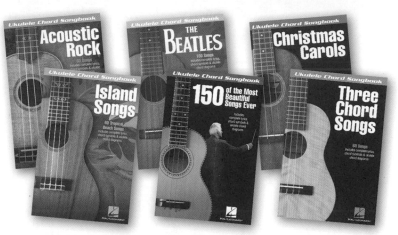

150 OF THE MOST BEAUTIFUL SONGS EVER

150 melodies: Always • Bewitched • Candle in the Wind • Endless Love • In the Still of the Night • Just the Way You Are • Memory • The Nearness of You • People • The Rainbow Connection • Smile • Unchained Melody • What a Wonderful World • Yesterday • and more.
00117051 . . . . $24.99

PETER, PAUL & MARY

Over 40 songs: And When I Die • Blowin' in the Wind • Goodnight, Irene • If I Had a Hammer (The Hammer Song) • Leaving on a Jet Plane • Puff the Magic Dragon • This Land Is Your Land • We Shall Overcome • Where Have All the Flowers Gone? • and more.
00121822 . . . . $14.99

THREE CHORD SONGS

60 songs: Bad Case of Loving You • Bang a Gong (Get It On) • Blue Suede Shoes • Cecilia • Get Back • Hound Dog • Kiss • Me and Bobby McGee • Not Fade Away • Rock This Town • Sweet Home Chicago • Twist and Shout • You Are My Sunshine • and more.
00702483 . . . . $15.99

TOP HITS

31 hits: The A Team • Born This Way • Forget You • Ho Hey • Jar of Hearts • Little Talks • Need You Now • Rolling in the Deep • Teenage Dream • Titanium • We Are Never Ever Getting Back Together • and more.
00115929 . . . . $14.99

Prices, contents, and availability subject to change without notice.

www.halleonard.com